UNEMPLOYMENT
AND THE MULTINATIONALS

UNEMPLOYMENT AND THE MULTINATIONALS

A Strategy for Technological Change in Latin America

DOUGLAS A. HELLINGER
STEPHEN H. HELLINGER

FOREWORD BY
BARBARA WARD

National University Publications
KENNIKAT PRESS   //   1976
Port Washington, N. Y.   //   London

Manufactured in the United States of America

Published by
Kennikat Press Corp.
Port Washington, N.Y./London

Library of Congress Cataloging in Publication Data

Hellinger, Douglas A
    Unemployment and the multinationals.

    (National university publications)
    Bibliography: p.
    Includes index.
    1. Labor supply—Latin America. 2. Technology
—Latin America. 3. International business enter-
prises. I. Hellinger, Stephen H., joint author.
II. Title.
HD5730.5.A6H44   331.1'1'098   76-8484
ISBN 0-8046-9126-6

TO ELEANOR, JIM, JOHN, AND BOB

CONTENTS

PREFACE

Peace Corps tours in Latin America provided the experiences and insights which made it increasingly difficult for us to accept the traditional attitudes and approaches of the international business community toward the Third World, given the pressing social and economic problems in those countries. A recognition of large-scale unemployment as one of the most serious of these problems provided the impetus for this book.

Unemployment, in Latin America and elsewhere, is but a symptom of a much more pervasive disease. Poverty rooted in exploitive political, economic, and social systems makes questions of local decision-making power and asset control the central issues in international development. Accordingly, appropriate technologies are those which not only can create new jobs in a labor-abundant economy, but those which can be understood and controlled at the local level for the satisfaction of self-determined needs.

Within such an approach to development there appears to be no place for giant multinational corporations which seek to optimize their international allocation of resources and maximize their profits. For the foreseeable future, however, these corporations will continue as major actors on the international scene. With this in mind, *Unemployment and the Multinationals* offers to the MNCs and to Latin American governments an alternative to a radical and perhaps violent resolution of one of the most urgent social problems in the Third World.

In the course of our research we benefited from the views and perspectives shared with us by a number of corporate executives, members of academia, and officials in international, U. S.–government, and nongovernment organizations. To those individuals we extend our gratitude.

PREFACE

In particular, we would like to thank Lady Jackson (Barbara Ward) and Neil Chamberlain for their assistance and encouragement, and Jack Baranson, whose friendship we have come to value as highly as his professional counsel. We are also especially grateful to Helen May, who deciphered and then typed our initial draft.

Finally, we wish to express our sincerest appreciation to a close friend and colleague, Anne Harrington, who, serving voluntarily as our much-needed editor, made substantial editorial and substantive contributions over the course of many weeks, and thus deserves major credit for the final version of this text.

FOREWORD

Each development decade has its "conventional wisdom." The
Fifties were concerned with the overriding need for economic growth, with
rapid industrialization as its main tool. In the Sixties, social issues such as
rising population pressure, the growth of unemployment, urban migration
and, towards the end, environmental constraints and the problem of income distribution—the constraints of justice—began to make their pressure
felt. By the Seventies, all these deeper issues started to come together in
"systems analyses" which, however, tended to lead in opposite directions—
the need for more economic growth with or without better social institutions producing one set of answers, the need for less growth to preserve the
integrity of the biosphere leading to a totally different constellation of
answers.

Perhaps we can hope that the rest of the Seventies will sort out the
muddle, suggesting not the supercession of systems but the need to see
them as a plural phenomenon, with different priorities and contexts for
different parts of the human community. The priority for economic
growth—still including unanalysed and uncured waste and induced
obsolescence—may be seen to be nil in countries with average per capita
income above, say, $2,000. But economic growth in the sense of genuine
productivity, the optimum use of resources (including abundant labour),
the opening up of new sources of energy and the careful re-use of all
materials susceptible of recycling—this may be seen to be a very high
priority indeed to the poorest lands.

But one of the great difficulties in adapting the right system to the
right area is that there is a continuous transmission belt of ideas, influences,

policies and investments between rich and poor regions and this belt can encourage not the best, but the worst, system for each. If the agencies of this transmission—public or private—do not give a quite new urgency to the appropriateness of their exchanges, the belt itself may become a chief cause of breakdown.

A concrete example is perhaps the best illustration. If a multinational corporation seeks to develop and secure raw materials from a poor country at the cheapest possible price while introducing the highest technology for their production, waste and over-use are encouraged in the wealthy investing nation while unemployment for the many and conspicuous consumption for the very few may be the local outcome. The total exchange, far from enhancing each community, produces the worst result for both. In short, all the agencies concerned with the world's economic interchanges have to invent and undertake the kind of "systems" approach which makes sure that transfers, investment decisions and social policies make sense *at both ends.*

Within such a context it is not inconceivable that multinational corporations, suitably regulated, could play a creative managerial role. But to do so, they need a new "systems" approach themselves. The value of this study is that it attempts in a very practical and concrete way to help forward the process of experiment and invention. Thus it deals with a key issue for the world economy's success or failure in the next twenty-five tumultuous years that are all that separate us from a new century and a world virtually twice as large as the one we have today.

BARBARA WARD

INTRODUCTION

When the 1970s become history, it is doubtful that Americans will express much sorrow. After a decade during which many hopes were raised and expectations generated, most of us are now fortunate if we can simply maintain the living standards that the economic growth of the 1960s bestowed upon us. At the same time, the minority of our population that has never shared in America's material abundance is being hardest hit by the phenomenon of "stagflation." Double-digit inflation and spiraling unemployment rates have become the central concerns of nearly all Americans. Indeed, the thought of double-digit *unemployment* figures conjures up images of the far more severe economic crisis of the 1930s and arouses our worst fears.

Yet between these two periods of economic crisis, while this country pursued policies that raised per capita income to unprecedented levels, the vast majority of Asians, Africans, and Latin Americans—and particularly those whose leaders chose to fashion their nations' development strategies on the growth-oriented models of the United States and Western Europe—did not share in the benefits of the postwar boom. Indeed, the proportion of the population that participated in their country's "development" in most cases actually decreased, as more and more people were unable to find jobs. Double-digit unemployment rates long ago became a reality in most Latin American countries. Even this measure, however, fails to reflect the gravity of the situation, for in Latin America and elsewhere in the Third World it is not uncommon to find those who are fully employed representing little more than one-half the total available labor force.

This figure reflects, in turn, an even more disturbing reality: families in the countryside underfed and undernourished because their members are unable to find work for months at a time. Heads of households forced to leave their families to supplement their incomes elsewhere. Large-scale and ever-increasing migration to the urban areas in search of more viable employment opportunities. Unfulfilled promises of jobs in the cities' factories. Competition with thousands of others seeking to service the privileged few. Unproductive, demeaning, infrequent, underpaid work. The degradation of constantly searching for and being denied a chance to earn a living. Frustration, anger, crime, violence. . .

The sad irony is that the energies of this underemployed labor force are of necessity finding their outlet in destructive or, at best, unproductive activities while, at the same time, these human capabilities represent the greatest potential resource for the development of the Third World. The more fully and rationally a nation's work force is employed, the more rapidly its economy will grow. As the benefits of this growth will thus be spread more equitably among its people, there will naturally be resistance from the heretofore favored segments of the population. The political obstacles to any attempt to redistribute income will be formidable, but a full-employment program, by increasing output, effecting a more just distribution of income, and stimulating consumer demand in one process offers the most acceptable and effective manner by which to bring about such a fundamental change.

This is not to say, however, that other, more difficult measures are not required if the goal of "growth with justice" is to be attained. Land and agrarian reform programs must be implemented to provide the incentive and the means by which the small farmer can demonstrate his highly productive capabilities. Similarly, small entrepreneurs must have access to credit and other services on the same favorable terms available to larger companies if they are to compete effectively. The countryside and the smaller towns must be made attractive places in which to live if the migratory flow to the major cities is not soon to reach such proportions that the problems it creates there become insoluble. This is not to imply that jobs should not also be created within the structures now existing in the large urban areas, or that efforts should not be made to increase the attractiveness of city life as well. Progress on both fronts will offer greater choice to the individual—a phenomenon that is the essence of development itself.

Higher income, more relevant education, increased participation, a larger number of alternatives, and a greater freedom of choice are the factors that can undermine the fatalistic attitudes that so commonly characterize the poor. The increased control one consequently feels and has over his or her life is an end sufficient in itself. Yet its ramifications can be equally profound. The desire to fulfill one's potential, once kindled, can become a society's most productive force. Furthermore, having children is less likely to remain central to personal fulfillment once other avenues to that fulfillment are open. Lower fertility rates and greater social and economic productivity, taken together, not only bode well for the development of the Third World but also offer an escape from our worst Malthusian nightmares.

The technologies commonly utilized, however, in economically productive activities in most of the developing world—and particularly in Latin America—have been antithetical to this development process. Machinery, techniques, and forms of organization that are not adequately understood by those whom they affect and that minimize their paticipation deprive people of the opportunity to control their own environment. As it incorporates the knowledge, experience, and values of another culture, transplanted technology, unless successfully adapted, is inimical to the conditions and needs of its new surroundings. To the extent that it does not make optimum use of all available resources and does not benefit all members of a society, it is inappropriate for that society's development.

In Latin America, and in the Third World in general, human resources are usually those which are least fully utilized. By using highly mechanized techniques, developed in the United States and Western Europe during periods of relative labor scarcity, these less developed countries are making costly expenditures on sophisticated machinery when human manpower can frequently accomplish the same tasks. Furthermore, the employment of these more labor-intensive techniques broadens the participatory base of the development effort and distributes the returns to productive activity more evenly throughout the society.

The term labor-intensive evokes images of back-breaking work, using the most primitive implements. This need not be, and indeed rarely is, the case. Between the most elementary technologies and those which are so highly automated that they regiment, bore, and alienate the worker lie a wide range of intermediate alternatives that complement and support rather than replace him. Craft activity is the most common example, but intermediate technologies are also appropriate on farms, in factories, in building a nation's rural infrastructure, and in constructing its cities. In these activities some boring, hard work is inevitable; it is part of any development process. Yet such technologies at least offer one a chance to work if he or she so wishes—a choice that is not afforded by the more capital-intensive production methods.

It is equally important that the more "modern" technologies, with the scale of operations and political and economic linkages generally associated with them, do not displace the labor-absorbing activities of small, indigenous enterprises and small-scale agriculture. These more traditional

[5]

endeavors, in addition to the employment they generate, are most compatible with local cultures and hold the greatest promise for increased productivity if they are supplied the necessary institutional and technical support.

The use of capital-intensive technologies is attributable to a host of political, economic, and educational factors. Most Third World engineers, economists, and businessmen, for example, are usually not exposed in the course of their training to alternative technologies—a miseducation that reflects and perpetuates the bias, particularly in Latin America, toward the newest and most sophisticated machinery. More often than not, a production technique is selected on the basis of imperfect information, leaving unconsidered a number of more appropriate possibilities. The role of the multinational corporation [MNC] as a transfer agent is particularly significant, as it generally introduces a technological package basically unadapted to local conditions.

The complementarity of the package's components frequently creates the need on the part of the recipient country for continued access to the resources of the MNC. The relationship of dependency that consequently evolves runs directly counter to the long-term development goals and interests of most Third World countries. Some constituents of these countries naturally gain from their association with such foreign interests and from a growth-oriented development strategy. If the MNC is courted by these privileged groups, its impact on political sovereignty, government policy, social institutions, and sociocultural values can be particularly significant. Furthermore, the foreign corporation, with the technologies it utilizes, can have adverse economic effects, particularly in the area of employment through the displacement of existing traditional enterprises and by the deterrent its presence represents to the establishment of such enterprises in the future.

This is not to say that the multinational corporation has not made contributions to the development effort by its transfer of resources, or that it is incapable of playing a more positive role. Yet it is not in the short-term corporate interest to adapt and share its technology for the purpose of resolving socioeconomic problems such as un- and underemployment. Indeed, the MNC will continue to produce with a relatively small work force both for a small, affluent class in the host country and for export. Hence, firm government action is required if there is to be any hope that the foreign corporation, as well as its domestic counterpart, will adapt its technologies so as to offer a far larger number of employment opportunities. In addition, Third World governments must provide incentives—including the creation of a rural infrastructure—that will encourage the decentralization of industrial activity and take jobs and services to people in their own localities.

MNCs will also have to respond, especially during this period of economic difficulties, to the increasing stream of criticism they will receive for exacerbating the unemployment and balance-of-payments problems of their home countries. A discussion of this critically important theme is conspicuously absent from this book, as is an examination of the larger questions of the international division of labor and the role of the transnational corporation in the international allocation of resources. As relevant as these subjects are, we felt compelled to omit them if we were to focus effectively on one vital issue in Latin America's development. For the same reason, we have made only passing reference to multilateral and bilateral foreign aid and trade and international monetary matters. A host of related issues, however, including the lowering of tariff barriers to the labor-intensively produced goods of the Third World and the covering of local as well as foreign exchange costs by foreign aid donors, must continue to be explored in other forums.

Our virtual neglect of labor-intensive technological possibilities in agriculture, construction, and other sectors, as well as the cursory nature of our review of the encompassing questions of industrial decentralization and rural-urban migration, should not be construed as signifying a lack of interest in, or importance attached to, these areas. Indeed, as has been emphasized in this Introduction, no employment program or any other government policy can be successfully pursued if it is not part of a broad development strategy. In this book, we concentrate on just one aspect of this strategy: the technological adaptations required to significantly reduce the high levels of joblessness that exist today in Latin America and the role of the multinational corporation in this endeavor.

Chapter I establishes the seriousness of the employment problem and the need to redirect current strategies of development.

Chapter II examines the labor-absorbing potential of the various economic sectors. The importance of directly generating additional employment in modern manufacturing is emphasized, and the means for doing so are suggested. The introduction of more labor-intensive technologies is viewed as essential.

Labor-intensive technological possibilities in the various manufacturing sectors and the scope for labor substitution in the different production processes are explored in Chapter III. The range of technological choice in a cross-section of industries is also examined.

In Chapter IV, the traditional emphasis on labor productivity is questioned and other economic considerations in the choice of technology, particularly those pertaining directly or indirectly to labor and capital costs, are reviewed.

Chapter V indicates the various ways that appropriate technologies can be obtained. The importance of undertaking research, development, and engineering efforts within Latin America is stressed and the institutions within which this work could be done are recommended. The suitability of MNC subsidiaries is emphasized.

What the MNC is currently doing, should be doing, and is capable of doing to generate employment in other fashions is the subject of Chapter VI. An investigation is made of the extent to which distorted factor prices and other economic considerations contribute to the MNC's selection of production methods, as well as of its capacity to respond constructively to the unemployment problem. The central issue is whether the MNC's sensitivity to this problem and its managerial flexibility match its impact on the local economy and its consequently high potential for assisting in an effort to create more jobs.

An examination is made in Chapter VII of the general approach of Latin American governments to the employment problem, technology, and the MNC, as well as of the policies of selected countries. Policy alternatives aimed at maximizing the contribution of the MNC to employment generation are suggested, and the corporation's response to possible government pressure is considered.

Finally, in Chapter VIII, our findings are summarized, conclusions are drawn, and a look into the future is attempted.

1 EMPLOYMENT AND DEVELOPMENT IN LATIN AMERICA

The deterioration of the human condition in Latin America is going to continue for the foreseeable future. Each year there will be more people. . . Between 1925 and 1960, the population doubled, from 100 million to 200 million. In 2000, it will be 600 million. . . Almost half of the 600 million people in the year 2000 will be surplus to the society's labor needs and absorptive capacity. . . The mind boggles at the projections, but they are projections based on precise statistics.[1]

In these few sentences, Gary MacEoin has captured the essence of the frightening reality that confronts Latin America. Increasingly rapid population growth, particularly since the 1940s, has swelled the ranks of the labor force as each generation comes of working age. Massive migration by the rural population in search of more viable employment opportunities in the cities only compounds the problem. This phenomenon has resulted in some of the highest un- and underemployment rates in the world—in both the urban and rural sectors—and there are few indications that there is much if any relief ahead.

MAGNITUDE OF THE PROBLEM

MacEoin paints a more detailed picture with some additional statistics. A population growth rate of 1.9 percent per annum during the second half of the 1930s grew to rates of 2.3 percent in the 1940s, 2.8 percent in the 1950s, and 2.9 percent during the 1960s, as death rates were continually lowered and birth rates remained high. But even these figures do not accurately reflect the magnitude of the problem. The populations of Argentina and Uruguay grew at rates of under 1.5 percent during the 1960s, while Chile and Cuba also registered relatively moderate increases. With these countries excluded, the population of Latin America as a whole is increasing by over 3 percent annually. In countries such as Ecuador and Colombia, the rates are as high as 3.5 percent; in the latter this fact is partially explained by a decline in deaths from near forty per thousand people in 1962 to close to thirty by the end of the decade. Bolivia and Peru have yet to experience such declines, and therefore their populations are not expanding so rapidly; when such expansion does occur, the magnitude of the continent's population problem will be even greater.[2]

It is beyond the scope of this book to explore the many difficulties involved in introducing an effective birth control program in Latin America. It is clear, however, that even if a significant reduction in births were to be achieved in the immediate future, it would have no effect on the size of the labor force for another fifteen to eighteen years while the already-born gradually join the ranks. The International Labour Office (ILO) points out[3] that the high fertility rates of recent years already assure an increase of more than 60 percent in Colombia's working age population between 1970 and 1985, during which time the active labor force will grow from about 6.5 million to almost 11 million. In Mexico, those born during the late 1950s and the 1960s will swell the labor ranks during this decade; it is predicted that in 1980 there will be 850,000 new entrants, as compared with 600,000 in 1970.[4] In fact, in countries in which birth rates reached their apex five to fifteen years ago, the increases in the labor forces over this decade will even be higher than the still large-scale increases in population.

The pattern holds for Latin America in general. Between 1950 and 1965, the growth of the labor force in South America (excluding Argentina and Uruguay) was 2.7 percent per year and in Central America, 2.8 percent. It is estimated[5] that during the 1970s the annual average will surpass 3 percent in both areas, cumulating, in some countries, in additions to the labor force of over 40 percent. These increases are not only high absolutely but are considerably higher than those expected in the world's other less developed regions.

Most of Latin America's labor force is becoming increasingly concentrated in the cities. Migration from the countryside continues unabated and, although these migrants do not necessarily bear the brunt of unemployment in their new setting,[6] they do place a serious strain on its overall absorption. This migration and rapid population growth combine to give Latin America a higher rate of urbanization than any other region in the world. In 1970, 54 percent of its population lived in urban areas, and it is projected that the figure will be 60 percent in 1980 and 80 percent by the end of the century.[7]

Brazil, with at least seven metropolitan areas with over one million inhabitants, including two of the world's largest cities, is a case in point. Today, over half its population is urbanized, and by 1990 the share should be in the area of 63 percent. In other words, within the next fifteen years, 100 million Brazilians will be living in cities. Of the 48 million in urban areas in 1970, nearly a third earned less than the legal minimum wage and could be considered un- or underemployed.[8] Many of the one million people who migrate each year from the countryside consitute part of those underemployment lists, as they must settle for part-time or menial jobs.

Open unemployment has risen rapidly during the past generation. The Organization of American States [OAS] estimates that the total number of unemployed in Latin America rose from more than 2.9 million in 1950 to more than 8.8 million in 1965, with a particularly large increase of more than 2.5 million during the first half of the 1960s. In 1965, over 11 percent of Latin Americans were fully unemployed, compared with just above 9 percent in 1960;[9] the open unemployment rate is now thought to be at least 13 percent.

These figures can be misleading, however, for they tend to understate the problem. As a family moves from the countryside to the city, its children of over fifteen years of age are no longer considered unemployed if they enter school, as is often the case. Their mother, who had earlier been considered part of the agricultural work force, may now become primarily a housewife. And their grandfather has a far better chance to find salaried employment offering retirement benefits which may take him out of the labor force when he becomes sixty.[10] Furthermore, those not seeking work during the prescribed time period are often not counted as unemployed. The relevancy of this last point for Latin America is borne out in studies cited by the International Labour Office, which report an inverse correlation between the level of unemployment and the tendency of people to seek jobs.[11]

Even with these factors taken into account, the figures cited still do not begin to measure the underutilization of available human resources. Erik Thorbecke measures "potential employment" or the "unemployment equivalent" by comparing the total number of man-hours actually worked to the available manpower resources expressed in man-hours per year. A 1969 OAS study using this approach reveals rates of combined un- and underemployment ranging from 20 to over 50 percent. Colin Bradford distinguishes between the percentage of people not fully employed—which he places at over 40 percent—and the proportion of available man-hours not utilized—which he calculates to have been approximately 27 percent, or 18 million people, in 1960.[12]

An ILO estimate that in 1970 only some 5 million man-years were being utilized out of an approximate labor capacity of 6.5 million man-years in Colombia accords with Bradford's finding. Most of the overt unemployment was located in the cities—approximately three-quarters of it, according to one study[13]—despite the fact that Colombia's population is still roughly half urban and half rural. In 1951 urban unemployment was in the area of 4 or 5 percent, but that figure has risen sharply to approximately 11 percent. It has been in the major cities that the unemployment problem has been most acute. In 1967, for example, rates reached 13 percent in Bogotá and Medellín, 15 percent in Cali, and over 18 percent in Barranquilla.[14]

Again, it need be emphasized that these statistics only measure the magnitude of *open* unemployment; that is, the proportion of persons seeking work unsuccessfully. Out of a potential labor force of some 3 million, at least one-half million fall into this category. A good many of these are people with some skills who are searching for opportunities in the modern sector. They are often the victims of labor legislation which, with management and labor union backing, serves to perpetuate unemployment in that sector by favoring the employment of existing work forces for longer hours over the enlistment of additional personnel. Furthermore, the relatively high wages offered in the modern sector often raise the aspirations of these job seekers and dissuade many from looking for employment in other sectors.

In the traditional sector, on the other hand, there are great amounts of underemployment. Here, much of the employment is on a noncontractual basis, including a large number of family operations. Thus, employers are free to divide a limited number of work opportunities among several people, with the result that partial employment is a prevalent condition. In addition, there are large portions of the labor force that spend their time engaged in activities such as street vending—activities that are inherently unstable and cannot be characterized as full-time occupations.

The ILO estimates that—based on the number of openly unemployed, partially employed, and those too discouraged to even seek work—shortage of work affects about one-quarter to one-third of the urban labor force. These levels are comparable to those reached in industrialized countries during the Depression of the 1930s and are probably even higher than those experienced in Colombia itself during that time. What is more discouraging is the rapid growth of the labor force and the slow growth in employment opportunities. By 1985, the country's work force will be close to 11 million, 8 million of whom will be in the cities. If, over the next twelve years, job creation does not exceed its present rate of less than 2.5 percent, there will be a total of 4 million un- and underemployed, most of whom will be in urban areas, where three-quarters of Colombia's population will then be living.[15]

Hence, if present trends continue, open urban unemployment in Columbia in 1985 may reach as high as 30 percent and those finding themselves short of, or without, work could very well constitute one-half of the country's urban labor force. Clearly, the very strong possibility that such an alarming situation will be realized requires a critical examination of the policies that have created this condition in so many Latin American nations.

RE-EVALUATION OF DEVELOPMENT STRATEGIES

Recently, Mahbub ul Haq of the World Bank characterized the basic approach to international economic development to which he and his colleagues elsewhere in the field subscribed throughout most of the postwar period. It is an approach that is being reconsidered today in light of the alarming levels of unemployment and skewed patterns of income distribution both present today and projected for the near future in Latin America. Wrote Haq:

... we conceived our task not as the eradication of the worst forms of poverty but as the pursuit of certain high levels of per capita income. We convinced ourselves that the latter is a necessary condition for the former but we did not in fact give much thought to the inter-connection. We development economists persuaded the developing countries that life begins at $1,000 and thereby we did them no service. They chased elusive per capita income levels, they fussed about growth rates in GNP . . . .[16]

Some countries have, in fact, attained those high growth rates, but without the forecasted consequences. During the 1950s, the gross national product of Venezuela increased at an annual rate of 8 percent, but the number of unemployed was greater at the end of the decade than at the beginning. Likewise, although industrial output tripled between 1950 and 1967, employment in that sector expanded by a total of only 66 percent— a rate of increase that did not even keep pace with the natural additions to the labor force.[17] Brazil, which has been growing in real terms at an average rate of about 10 percent over the past few years and whose annual industrial growth has been on the order of 14 percent, today has a smaller proportion of its population gainfully employed than it did two decades ago.[18] And in the case of Mexico, the GNP and unemployment have been growing at the same 6 to 7 percent annual rate for the past fifteen years.[19]

It appears that if a policy of rapid growth is going to be pursued, rates considerably higher than those achieved by Mexico must be attained if even the annual increases to the labor force are to be absorbed. Given the difficulties involved in increasing output in the agricultural sector by more than 5 percent yearly, a "growth first" government would have to strive for increases in industrial growth even higher than those achieved thus far by Brazil in order even to begin making a dent in the backlog of its unemployed.

A heavy emphasis upon modern industry, while perhaps generating rapid growth, does not necessarily generate employment. In fact, the more likely consequence is the development of a small middle class with rising incomes and the confinement of the vast majority of workers to the lists of the unemployed, underemployed, or to practically subsistence-wage occupations. This is the result of the introduction of increasing amounts of capital per laborer, thereby raising the latter's productivity and hence his wages. Meanwhile, not only are many potential workers left on the outside, not reaping the benefits of the industrial growth, but modern industries also entice large numbers of rural workers while eliminating through competition many of their potential sources of employment in the traditional urban sector.

This phenomenon has received particular mention in the cases of Brazil by World Bank President Robert McNamara, Colombia by the ILO, and Mexico by James Grant, President of the Overseas Development Council. Over a ten-year period, the income of Mexico's landless laborers fell by 15 percent, while that of its modern factory workers rose by about 20 percent. "Thus, in Mexico," Grant concludes, "as in most of Latin America, the people for whom the system has been working so far—a sizable group that includes civil servants and industrial workers—are doing very well. But for a sizable and growing portion of the population at the bottom, there has been little progress and in many cases their situation is getting even worse."[20]

Furthermore, both Grant and Haq emphasize the difficulties that arise when attempts are made to redistribute income in favor of those who were for the most part left out of the productive process. The realities of economic and political life today, particularly in Latin America, are such that those in possession of the lion's share of their country's wealth are most unlikely to allow such a redistribution. The mechanisms for this process, particularly fiscal policy, even when given some opportunity to operate, have shown their general ineffectiveness. In Uruguay, for example, the continent's most progressive welfare programs have necessitated heavy taxation and reductions in the amounts of capital available for investment, thereby contributing heavily to both higher levels of unemployment and the stagnation in economic growth. On the other hand, in countries—such as Brazil and Mexico—that do not emphasize the redistribution of the benefits of their rapid growth, the gap between the small, wealthy classes and large segments of the population outside the modern sector is widening at a steadily increasing pace.

Lloyd Reynolds and Peter Gregory, in their study of the industrial development of Puerto Rico,[21] illustrate what happens to a labor-abundant country that hopes to eliminate unemployment through a policy of rapid modernization. Puerto Rico has had a high rate of growth in per capita output since the early 1940s, and in about 1950 was roughly comparable to Brazil and Colombia today in terms of both per capita income and the percentages of the labor force and net income in manufacturing. Throughout the 1950s, very favorable circumstances prevailed for industrial growth, including heavy imports of capital, technology, and management. In addition, a "tax holiday" law and the creation of an industrial promotion program, which included finanacial incentives to modern plants, provided an attractive investment environment.

As a result, there has been rapid expansion of industrialization and wealth on the island. Nevertheless, unemployment has not fallen markedly, and during periods of slackening migration to the mainland (as in the early 1960s) the percentage of unemployed has actually risen. If, during a period in which so many elements conducive to an economic boom are present—as was the case from 1950 to 1962—only some 115,000 jobs were created, what hope would there be for absorbing the 40,000 workers who would enter the labor force annually if net migration to the mainland were zero?

That which is true of Puerto Rico is also applicable to Latin America in general. That is, most of the governments are attempting to follow the pattern of development established by the now industrially advanced countries, despite the fact that in Latin America, unlike in the advanced countries at a comparable period in time, population growth rates are still high. And in spite of the consequently large labor pools, economic policies are not geared to take advantage of this abundantly available, relatively inexpensive factor of production.

Reorienting a nation's productive capacity to fully utilize the vast quantity of human resources at its disposal should, unlike most current policies, both accelerate growth and assure a fairer distribution of income throughout the populace. The ILO, in its report on Colombia, emphasized this point, stating that:

... unemployment need not necessarily be considered a burden for policy makers. It can be looked on as a potential asset. To treat it as a liability is one indication of how one's values become distorted during a period of large-scale unemployment. There is this reserve of human resources available, if only the will and the way could be found to mobilize them for national development; certainly the long-term outlook for reaching high living standards would be in some ways more bleak if there were neither spare labour nor spare land to be brought into production.[22]

As discussed earlier, even a moderate redistribution of income is difficult to achieve in most places on the continent owing to structural rigidities. While those employed in the modern sector usually receive considerable fringe benefits, the common absence of any nation-wide social security program places an additional handicap on the underemployed and low-wage earners. The usual result is an increasing reliance upon the family for support. Yet the urban family is not always as available or capable of fulfilling this function as its rural counterpart traditionally is. The problem is compounded as the ranks of unemployed youth increase. The difficulties that those in their late teens and early twenties have in finding gainful employment create a situation in which each worker must support a growing number of dependents.

Government investments in social services, especially education of the young, are often wasted if their beneficiaries are not given the opportunity to exploit them for socially productive ends. In fact, it can be argued[23] that prolonged unemployment has economic costs in that the value of human capital depreciates the longer that it is disassociated from its once familiar task. Inversely, jobs themselves can provide training and skills that are not available to people from other sources.

If jobs are found for the currently un- and underemployed, it cannot be assumed that their recipients will not be capable of saving. Today's low savings levels among Latin America's poorer classes may be due, in large part, to the absence of adequate and accessible savings institutions. Indeed, if programs were designed that would demonstrate to the worker the benefits that derive in the short term from his saving (e.g., a housing scheme), the results might dispel a great many fears that increasingly larger returns to labor rather than to capital would seriously hamper investment. A recent study of Asian countries shows that a more equal distribution of income actually can increase net savings,[24] as they are more frequently invested directly or indirectly in productive domestic activities. On the other hand, returns on capital often wind up in the hands of parent foreign companies, in Swiss bank accounts, or in speculative land purchases.

There is another economic reason for increasing employment immediately, even if it might mean postponing high growth rates. Highly skewed income patterns stimulate an excessive demand for sophisticated engineering products—goods that possess a relatively high capital and foreign exchange content. Consequently, domestic production opportunities are lost, and those that remain within the country cannot offer a great deal of employment.

As the urban middle class grows in size, greater expenditures will be made on these sophisticated manufactured goods vis-a-vis wage goods. Between 1950 and 1965, for example, per capita income rose at an annual rate of 2.5 percent, while per capita consumption of foodstuffs increased yearly by only 1.1 percent.[25] This contrast indicates a vast potential market for agricultural goods—as well as for labor-intensive products such as clothing—which could be fully exploited if only enough of the national product were in the hands of those who today cannot yet afford sufficient amounts of life's necessities. The benefits that would accrue if such a change could be effected would be enormous: the retention of greater numbers of rural workers on the farm to produce the increased quantities of foodstuffs demanded and the creation of many more factory jobs for the manufacture of greater amounts of labor-intensive products.

Perhaps of even greater long-range consequence is the delimiting effect that major increases in employment can have on population growth. An interesting study by William Rich[26] shows that, wherever modern goods and services are distributed equitably to a large majority of the population, national birth rates have fallen significantly, even before large-scale family planning programs are initiated. As examples, Rich cites countries from all parts of the world, including, in Latin America, Costa Rica and Uruguay, contending that while religious and cultural variables do affect attitudes toward family size, similar approaches in different religious and cultural settings have roughly comparable effects on fertility rates.

On the other hand, practically every less developed country whose national income is not broadly distributed still has high birth rates—regardless of how rapidly the country is growing in economic terms. Mexico and Venezuela illustrate the point. In 1970, the former had a per capita income comparable to those of Uruguay and Chile, two countries whose socioeconomic benefits were far more widely distributed than those in Mexico. In that year the birth rates in Uruguay and Chile were well under thirty per thousand of the population, while Mexico's was over forty. Likewise Argentina, which has had a GNP per capita as large as, and a distribution of income and services far better than those in Venezuela, has had to contend with a birth rate only one-half as high as the latter's.

Although declining fertility rates are usually more closely correlated to rising education levels than to any other one variable, and despite the sundry manners in which goods and services can reach larger segments of the population, vastly increased employment opportunities appear the key to curtailing rapid population growth. It is employment, by generating sufficient income, that enables a poor family to take advantage of the educational opportunities that may be available. It is the income from good jobs that makes it possible for a family to supply its children with the health care and nutritional diet without which an education might be of little value. It is also assurance of gainful and lasting employment that reduces the feeling of insecurity and thus the perception of children as providers both in the short run and in one's old age.

The factor of greatest significance, however, may be the feeling of a greater control over one's fate that permanent employment can foster within an individual. Among a people whose traditional approach to life has been largely fatalistic, such a change can have very positive consequences, not only for limiting population increases but for the total national development effort as well. Among women, such a change in attitude may have a particularly potent effect. Without hope or even knowledge of alternative life circumstances, child-bearing and child-rearing often become central to a woman's enjoyment and self-perceived role in life.

If a woman can find a job that takes her outside the home environment, there is great potential for a new awareness to develop. This is particularly true if the work differs clearly from the traditional female role and provides the woman an income sufficient to increase her feeling of independence and to attach a significant opportunity cost to having children.[27] In addition, those alterations of the female role to which increased employment opportunities may contribute and which lead gradually to a modification of traditional cultural patterns may constitute in the long run the most effective means by which to resolve the overpopulation dilemma in Latin America.

Present indications are, however, that jobs for women,[28] particularly women of child-bearing age, are not abundantly available. The ILO's study of open unemployment in Colombia in 1967[29] reveals that a full 63 percent of the women unemployed were between the ages of 15 and 24. The proportion is similar in the case of males: the same age group accounted for over half the total number of men unemployed. By contrast, in the same year, men between 15 and 24 constituted roughly only a quarter of the occupied urban labor force. To look at this phenomenon from another viewpoint, over one-fourth of the young people available for employment in Colombia's cities are openly unemployed.

The greater the number of disappointments encountered by youth as they seek employment, the less productive they will be both socially and economically later in life. Failure tends to become self-sustaining and leads to feelings of resignation and apathy. As the ILO spells out, the consequences can be more far-reaching:

There is no escape from the psychological damage of unemployment—the demoralizing daily round looking for work, and the even more demoralizing series of refusals, increasing a man's disillusionment with himself and with society as the months tick by, and undermining the family's respect for him as an individual. Thousands of women and young girls are compelled to prostitute their bodies to support themselves and their dependents.[30]

Future employers may pay the price of this psychological damage incurred earlier as a result of unemployment. They may also have to deal with these apathetic feelings, if not sentiments of bitterness and resentment.

Interviews with hundreds of professionals in the New York area in 1932 (at which time unemployment figures in the United States and in its large cities were comparable to those in Latin America and its urban areas today) revealed the depth of feeling that a sudden disintegration of security can produce.[31] Similar to young people in the countryside who leave the familiarity of their rural homes to seek opportunities in the city but find only the uncertainties of city life, these men were also struggling with the insecurities that unemployment creates. Their general attitude was to blame those they felt were responsible for denying their desires for security: the employing class, the economic system, the government, or in some cases, all agencies of the existing order.

Despite obvious differences between these two sets of circumstances, there is no reason to believe that the young unemployed in Latin America are not developing similar attitudes. As their feelings of frustration and bitterness grow and the worth of their education and skills deteriorate through disuse, their value as potential employees also diminishes. Yet the consequences of unemployment may not take so long to materialize. If full employment is not soon given top priority in government policies, the too-often frustrated may very well seek their own violent solution to the problem.

SUMMARY

The record in Latin America over the past three decades illustrates the futility of waiting for high industrial growth rates to lead to meaningful development. Today, as national labor forces and populations increase at rates of over 3 percent each year and cities bulge with evergrowing numbers of the un- and underemployed, it is more imperative than ever to depart from conventional development thinking. For the benefits of growth to be enjoyed by more than just a small portion of these growing populations, strategies must be established and implemented to increase employment significantly in all sectors of the economy. Today's underutilized human resources must be looked upon as assets rather than liabilities; their employment should contribute to growth, not stifle it. And in those cases in which some growth must be sacrificed in the short run as jobs are created and dislocations occur, the loss will in no way compare with the long-term economic and social benefits that such a reorientation of policy will bring.

2 MODES OF LABOR ABSORPTION

A full-employment strategy implies that national resources must be directed toward finding employment for the millions of un- and underemployed
throughout the continent. It implies that employment should be a priority and not a by-product of the pursuit of other goals. Furthermore, it implies that the commitment be total and immediate, with the burden not
falling exclusively upon any one sector of the economy. Yet even among
those who identify the employment question as the most serious in Latin
America today, there are many who see the responsibility for labor absorption limited to only one or two sectors. Others argue that it is more realistic to expect significant job creation to occur indirectly rather than through
the use of direct methods, particularly when the latter involve a change in
production technologies. In this chapter, a case is made for the necessity
to develop new job opportunities in the manufacturing sector and the need
to do so through the introduction of more labor-intensive production processes.

SECTORAL CAPACITY FOR LABOR ABSORPTION

The magnitude of the employment problem is too great to ignore
the absorptive capacity of any economic sector. Agriculture has the potential to absorb a great deal of the pool of underemployed in the region, but
some very basic institutional changes are necessary. Foremost on the list
is the need for comprehensive policies of land redistribution, accompanied
by an effective program of agricultural services extended to the small farmer. Principally for political reasons, few such policies have been implemented, however, and fewer still have been successful. Ultimately, land reform

may be the most effective, if not only, way to rectify inequities and stimulate development in the agricultural sector, but presently in most Latin American countries, the prospect of this sector providing a significant increase in employment is dim.

Recent trends, in fact, have been disappointing. Between 1950 and 1965, agricultural employment in the region increased by only 1.5 percent annually and agriculture's share of the total labor force fell from 50 to 43 percent and then to 42 percent by the end of the decade.[1] In Colombia, where the figure was 45 percent in 1970, agriculture was providing only about 30,000 additional jobs annually.[2] When this figure is contrasted with the need for some 4 million new jobs in that country by 1985, it becomes clear that the agricultural sector alone cannot resolve the unemployment problem.

Indeed, the prospect is that the situation will grow worse in most countries. Little effort has been expended toward developing appropriate, labor-intensive technologies, and the high substitutability of capital for labor in this sector[3] poses the real danger that increasing mechanization and productivity will continue to release agricultural manpower. Concurring with this observation, Raul Prebisch also points out that perceived opportunities and other attractions of city life create an urban pull, which accelerates the rural push off the land.[4]

If nonagricultural employment can be created in the rural areas, the flow of the jobless to the large cities can be slowed. The decentralization of industry would contribute significantly in this respect, but basic infrastructure is a prerequisite. Rural works programs, while limited in the number of long-term, full-time jobs they create, can construct, improve, and maintain the facilities for rural industrial production and employment. Works projects that improve the quality of the land and expand cultivable acreage also increase the demand for agricultural labor. Without such integrated programs, the outlook—a realistic one at this juncture— is that population and unemployment levels will be of crisis proportion in the large urban areas of the continent. In any event, the nonfarming sector's ability to absorb labor will become increasingly critical to any employment strategy.

The urban sector, however, has failed to absorb labor at rates anywhere near fast enough. Between 1945 and 1960, the economically active population in the sector had averaged an annual growth of only 3.9 percent, while urban populations on the continent were growing at 4.3 percent a year.[5] This trend continued through the 1960s, with the industrial group (consisting of manufacturing, mining, and construction) particularly delinquent in absorbing the surplus labor. It was taking in workers at an annual rate of less than 3 percent between 1950 and 1965[6] and, by the end of the decade, it was employing less than 20 percent of the total labor force in Latin America. An equally significant fact is that this proportion has been steadily declining—a trend which contrasts with that experienced by Western countries at similar stages of their own development.[7]

By 1969, industry was absorbing only 31 percent, or less than a third, of the total nonagricultural labor force in Latin America—as compared with 35 percent in 1950. This average was bolstered by figures of over 40 percent in Argentina and Mexico (as of 1965), but more indicative of trends in the region was Brazil. Industry's share of the Brazilian urban labor force fell from 31.6 percent to 24.3 percent between 1950 and 1965[8] and, during the second half of the decade, the number of industrial jobs increased at an annual rate of only 2.8 percent, representing little improvement over previous increases.

The result is that the service sector has become a refuge for an overgrown urban labor force, mopping up many of those who would otherwise be unemployed. That is not to say that there is not a high degree of underemployment in this sector. There are great amounts of labor redundancy in government, commerce, transport, domestic help, and other services that soak up urban workers, and productivity levels are extremely low.[9] But services have had to steadily increase their absorption of the urban work force in order to keep the level of overt unemployment within manageable bounds. Entering the 1970s, one out of every three Latin American workers (and some 51 percent of all Latin American urban laborers) were already employed in the service sector—an alarmingly high percentage for the general level of development in the region.

Some look to the service sector to absorb even more workers, but its proportion of labor absorption has already increased a full 10 percent since 1950.[10] Brazil again is a good case in point. In 1960, one-third of the working population was in the service sector; a decade later, the percentage had grown by 5 percent. Likewise, in Colombia, the proportion has almost reached 35 percent.[11] And, throughout the continent, much of this work consisted of marginal activities and underemployment. Clearly, the service sector is no panacea for job creation.

Nor is the construction sector. Some point to construction, public works, and other infrastructure programs as keys to any employment strategy but, as already indicated, there are some very real limitations. This is not to deny the merits of a labor-intensive construction program. More labor-intensive techniques are available—though not always used—and labor is most easily substituted for capital in this sector, in large part because the final product does not have to compete internationally.[12] The ILO has urged the Colombian government to adopt such techniques, because they will probably still be able to remain competitive in this area and also because the expected 2 percent growth rate in productivity is considered satisfactory.[13] In addition, this activity requires a great deal of unskilled labor.

However, it can be argued from several different perspectives that an overreliance on construction activities yields disappointing results. Those who place emphasis upon growth and productivity stress that construction and infrastructure help alleviate unemployment only in the short run and that an economy cannot sustain itself on the expansion of such unproductive sectors.[14] At the same time, those who give priority to job creation in the short run should recognize the limitations in this area. The ILO points to the "major part" the construction sector can play in a Colombian full-employment strategy, suggesting a rise of one-third in the construction industry's share of total employment. As that share stood at only 5.3 percent in 1970, however, such an increase alone would reduce the unemployment figure only slightly.

Another reason for not relying upon construction to alleviate the unemployment problem is that it fails to provide steady employment. This contention is supported by the ILO study of Colombia, which reported that in 1967, while 6 percent of all urban workers were engaged in construction, 12 percent of the unemployed urban workers had previously been employed in that activity. No other sector contributed as much to unemployment in this sense. All things considered, therefore, construction has its part to play in job creation, but its limitations indicate that major solutions to the unemployment problem must be found elsewhere.

Both the ILO report and an earlier study of Colombia[15] identify the artisan sector as a potentially strong area for employment expansion. Its capacity to absorb labor is greater than that of modern industry, because its methods of production are more labor-intensive. It was found, however, that while artisan manufacturing employed almost twice as many people as did industrial manufacturing, this sector was being largely neglected in the country's development plans.[16] Partly as a result of that neglect, artisan employment increased at an annual rate of only 1.8 percent in Colombia between 1950 and 1965—about average for Latin America during that time span.[17] The principal cause of this stagnation is structural and evolutionary, with factory production steadily displacing craft activity over the past fifty years. While efforts to stimulate the artisan sector through effective credit programs and improvement in marketing and technical services are imperative, trends confirm that factory production has an ever-increasing role to play in employment generation.

In a study published by the United Nations Economic Commission for Latin America (ECLA),[18] Latin America's position in 1965 was likened to that of the more advanced European countries a century earlier. In both cases, the artisan sector was very large, while factory employment was still limited but growing rapidly. The similarities end there, according to the report:

The growth of the European cities kept pace with the upsurge of industry. Manufacturing employment—mainly in the factory sector—and construction employment came to represent half, or more than half, of total urban employment. By contrast, Latin American cities have developed autonomously; industrial employment represents approximately one-third of urban employment, and often even less (it should be remembered that in Latin America the factory sector absorbs a smaller proportion of industrial employment than it does in Europe).

A year later, ECLA made the following projection:

The marked tendency registered in the past for artisan employment to be superseded, in relative terms, by employment in manufacturing industry proper will still be strongly in evidence in the near future. This might mean that during the next 10 or 15 years, the share of factory employment in total industrial employment might reach about 60 percent, which in turn would imply that of the 4.9 million additional workers joining the industrial labour force, only 1.2 million would go to increase the numbers employed in artisan industry, while employment in manufacturing activities proper would have to expand by 3.7 million, i.e., by 76 percent in relation to present levels.[19]

That is the scope of the problem and the extent of the responsibility of the factories of the continent.

The manufacturing sector cannot escape this responsibility for two reasons. The first is that it has been making an increasing contribution to the region's total output (its present share is near 25 percent), while displacing artisan production. Second, by generating income well above that produced by most of the rest of the economy, this sector has also been generating migration to the urban centers. An observer of the Colombian situation expressed the problem thus:

Quite naturally, there is a preference within the labor force to seek employment in high-productivity activities with relatively high wage levels. The question in developing countries is not so much how rapidly total employment will expand, but rather how rapidly will modern industries and services be able to expand the proportion of the total labor force which they employ.[20]

The factories of Latin America are now confronted with the difficult challenge of providing work for the growing numbers of today's urban jobless and tomorrow's rural migrants.

So far, that challenge has not been met. During the 1950s, total manufacturing employment in most of the countries of the region grew considerably less than one-half as fast as total output in the sector. Argentina experienced an actual decline in employment, while the number employed in manufacturing in Mexico remained about the same. In Brazil, during the same period, employment in manufacturing increased by only 2.6 percent annually, while urban populations were exploding at a yearly rate of 5.4 percent. This was in keeping with the postwar trends in Latin America, where urban populations were growing over 50 percent faster than jobs were being created in manufacturing. Even the growth rate of the total nonagricultural work force was 40 percent higher than that of manufacturing employment.[21]

The 1960s witnessed little change in this situation. Between 1961 and 1966, output continued to increase twice as fast as employment in both light and heavy manufacturing. Annual employment growth rates were only 2 and 3 percent, respectively. By the latter part of the decade, manufacturing was still employing approximately the same proportion of the active labor forces as in the early 1950s.[22] The present figure for countries like Ecuador, Venezuela, and Colombia is approximately 13 percent. More than half of this labor in Colombia is engaged in artisan activities, although artisan employment has dropped almost 3 percent as a share of total national employment since 1964. In the meantime, the percentage of jobs found in the factories, while not decreasing, has only remained constant[23] because of a slow rate of labor absorption. A decade ago, 10,000 such jobs were being created a year, but recently even that low figure has declined.[24] As a result, it is estimated that today only 325,000 permanent jobs exist in the modern industrial sector.

The ILO is not very confident about the prospects of job creation in the manufacturing sector in Colombia. It cites, on the one hand, a slow increase in the demand for the products of traditional industries and a slow rate of import substitution, and notes, on the other, an increased capital-intensivity. The fastest technological growth in Latin America has been in the manufacturing sector. A reversal must take place, for this sector must at least triple its labor absorption in order to take in 25,000 new workers a year:

Without rapid growth in the industrial sector, the Colombian economy will not be able to solve the employment problem. . . . More specifically, the manufacturing sector will have to absorb a bigger proportion of the labour force, and this means that its rate of expansion must be much faster than during recent years, and that the number of jobs it creates per unit of investment must be higher.[25]

A Rand Corporation research team also studied the Colombian economy and similarly concluded that "the pace at which employment opportunities . . . expand in urban communities will be in large part determined by how, and how fast, the manufacturing sector develops."[26] Manufacturing output has increased steadily in Colombia and even more rapidly in other countries such as Brazil, where industrial growth rates have averaged more than 12 percent annually over the past half dozen years. What is now required is growth of a more labor-intensive nature.

INDIRECT EMPLOYMENT EFFECTS OF MODERN MANUFACTURING

An additional question must be asked regarding the extent of the responsibility of the modern manufacturing sector in employment creation within Latin America. Do manufacturing firms have only a limited obligation in direct job creation in light of their indirect employment effects? Typical of the responses received to this question in interviews with international business executives was the contention of one company president that every direct labor job in his industry led to four or five indirect jobs through forward and backward linkages and through the generation of income, which creates demand for additional production.

This figure is cited by a variety of sources, but with little apparent substantiation. Expanded manufacturing production, regardless of the investor's nationality, enlarges the market for production inputs and may also contribute new supply inputs to other companies. In this sense, additional jobs, in fact, are created, but the linkages and jobs are not necessarily established domestically. There is also good reason to believe that the amount of indirect employment generation may be significantly reduced in many cases by high levels of traditional job displacement caused by competition from modern manufacturing.

It is also not necessarily true that this production must be of a capital-intensive (that is, highly mechanized or even automated) nature in order to maximize local linkages. In Puerto Rico, for example, the employment multiplier effect in construction has been found to be substantial, and construction is inherently a more labor-intensive activity than manufacturing. At the same time, the multiplier is small in the case of machinery and equipment production, because a high percentage of their components must be imported. Open economies, like those of Puerto Rico and the countries of Latin America, have substantially lower employment multipliers than countries that import relatively little.[27] A similar line of argument contends that the traditional manufacturing sector tends to draw upon the domestic capital goods producing sector, whereas modern industries require imported capital goods.[28] One would then have to seriously question the validity of any general statement to the effect that labor-intensive production, as a rule, calls forth fewer locally produced inputs than does more sophisticated production. That is not to say that there is not room for more import substitution in the form of input-producing industries. The potential for the growth of intermediate goods industries in support of the expansion of heavy industrial sectors has been noted.[29] In some of the more industrially advanced countries of the region, such as Brazil and Mexico, effective subcontracting systems have developed and have been of particular benefit to the automotive industry.[30] The Japanese, as part of their development process, established "cottage industries" to supply their modern industrial sector. These small plants, using labor-intensive methods, provided components and parts for modern production, which became increasingly more capital-intensive. A somewhat similar system now exists in the Peoples' Republic of China, where village industries are linked to larger factories and other industrial installations.[31]

Employment opportunities also can be expanded indirectly through increased income generation but, as with linkages, it is not at all clear that capital-intensive production is most effective in creating new jobs in this manner. Such production tends to engage relatively few workers at relatively high wages. A more careful analysis indicates that labor-intensive production contributes more in this area. The number of workers, and hence consumers, is increased and the type of products they buy becomes more labor-intensive in nature. These unskilled and semiskilled laborers receive relatively low pay and tend to buy the more basic, traditional products. As a result, further labor-intensive production is stimulated and higher levels of employment are generated.

Expansion of manufacturing production also creates greater employment opportunities in the service sector. A decade ago, Walter Galenson,[32] referring to developing countries in general, wrote:

... too little attention has been paid to those sectors of the economy in which the bulk of the new jobs are likely to be located, namely, commerce and services. This does not mean that manufacturing is unimportant; on the contrary, it is, in my estimation, the key sector for economic growth. Under the conditions of modern technology, however, its role is not likely to be that of a major source of new employment. Rather, it will tend to generate the effective demand leading to employment expansion in other sectors. This multiplier effect is apt to be much more significant than any direct contributions that the manufacturing sector can make to the alleviation of mass unemployment.

He suggests that "for every additional hundred workers in manufacturing there may well be a substantial multiple of this number added to the labour force in commerce, construction, transportation, and services . . . ." Galenson further points out that "a modern economy seems to require a certain minimum superstructure of commercial, governmental, and other services to support manufacturing; that is, there may well be certain fixed technological relationships between jobs in manufacturing and supporting services elsewhere." Those relationships may depend upon a variety of factors, including the initial size of the manufacturing sector, its relative productivity, the technique of production used, the degree of development of a country, and the size of its service sector.

Galenson and others[33] argue that the use of more capital-intensive techniques will lead to greater indirect employment in the tertiary sector, which will more than offset lower direct industrial employment. Galenson's concept of labor-intensivity, however, appears to be the use of greater amounts of labor without changing production techniques. Having made that assumption, he then points to lower productivity per worker and a constant manufacturing output and concludes that little additional tertiary employment will be created.

It is curious that productivity is measured in terms of labor in regions where human resources are abundant and usually quite cheap. Obviously, labor productivity will decline as workers are substituted for equipment to produce the same product and output in a more labor-intensive fashion. Within such a context, a ratio between employment in manufacturing and that created in services is meaningless. If one industrial job indirectly creates five service jobs, six new jobs are created; if two jobs of a more labor-intensive nature lead to five service jobs, the total is seven. The ratio has been halved, but employment has been increased absolutely. There is no indication that the same amount of output produced by more machines would necessarily lead to more jobs in the tertiary sector than would that produced by large numbers of workers. In fact, Galenson grants that even new manufacturing employment independent of increased output (i.e., in make-work positions) would certainly result in an increased demand for additional employees in commerce and services. That total output is sacrificed in most cases through the use of labor-intensive techniques is not proven conclusively by Galenson.

It is also very doubtful that there exists as much room for expansion of employment in the tertiary sector in Latin America as has been suggested for developing countries as a whole. Werner Baer and Michel Hervé have written that " . . . a fairly developed country might have a substantially expanded service sector; thus additional investment in the manufacturing sector will call forth relatively small amounts of increased service employment."[34] Because the service sector in most of Latin America is already as large as that in more developed countries, the amount of additional labor it can absorb may be very limited. Until the contrary can be established, reliance upon direct industrial employment should be increased.

Finally, there is the important question of the displacement by large-scale, modern factories of labor-intensive enterprises, including artisans, craftsmen, and their suppliers. It has been observed that one factory worker can do the work of, and thus replace, up to ten people employed in the artisan sector.[35] This may be a conservative figure in light of the following case, reported by Keith Marsden of the ILO:

One country imported two plastic injection-moulding machines costing $100,000 with moulds. Working three shifts and with a total labor force of forty workers they produced 1.5 million pairs of plastic sandals and shoes a year. At $2 a pair these were better value (longer life) than cheap leather footwear at the same price. Thus, 5,000 artisan shoemakers lost their livelihood; this, in turn, reduced the markets for the suppliers and makers of leather, hand tools, cotton thread, tacks, glues, wax and polish, eyelets, fabric linings, laces, wooden lasts and carton boxes, none of which was required for plastic footwear. As all the machinery and the material ... for the plastic footwear had to be imported, while the leather footwear was based largely on indigenous materials and industries, the net result was a decline in both employment and real income within the country.[36]

Estimating indirect employment effects is, at best, a difficult task. It is not at all clear that the multiplier effect of increased manufacturing output upon employment is as great as proponents of capital-intensive technology make it out to be. Even many of those who contend that greater employment will be generated in the long run concede that the expansion of modern, highly mechanized production may well have negative effects on employment in the short term. Yet it cannot be ruled out that even in the long run the so-called multiplier effect may often be zero or even negative.[37]

DIRECT EMPLOYMENT EXPANSION IN MANUFACTURING

It is therefore clear that neither indirect effects of modern manufacturing nor any other sector by itself can resolve Latin America's employment problem. There is thus a major role for the region's industry to play in providing work opportunities directly for the jobless. Three general means exist for the expansion of such opportunities: factor proportions of labor and capital can be adjusted in the production process, the product mix can be altered, and an attempt can be made to expand markets, including export markets. Pursuit of all three of these goals can be quite compatible in most instances.

The utilization of more labor-intensive industrial techniques is seriously questioned by proponents of growth-oriented development, who view "modernization" as a necessity in most industries to assure plant efficiency and quality control. More moderate critics also reject an approach that emphasizes the use of such appropriate technology, arguing that its availability is limited (an argument refuted in Chapter III) and that a change in production processes, in and of itself, can have only a marginal impact on labor absorption. On the other hand, they do recognize the potential effect of a policy that sets out to combine an introduction of more labor-intensive technologies with changes in the product mix and the expansion of markets, both domestic and foreign.

Apart from efforts to modify or alter production techniques in existing industries, any shift in production toward inherently more labor-intensive goods would be a major contribution to an employment program. The following description of the possibilities has great relevance for Latin America:

There is considerable scope in the less developed countries for a choice of more labor-intensive products for meeting the requirements of domestic consumers, apart from possibilities of export. Needs for basic wage goods (food, clothing, and housing) could be satisfied, for instance, by hand-pounded rice instead of milled rice, handwoven cloth instead of machine-made textiles, wooden or brick houses instead of reinforced concrete structures, and so on. Thus, an appropriate product mix could, up to a point defined by the market characteristics of each product, stimulate greater employment without sacrificing output.[38]

The trend in postwar Latin America, however, has been in the opposite direction. As manufacturing output has grown steadily, it has shifted away from the traditional sectors and toward the skill- and capital-intensive industries. Manufacturing employment has not increased significantly and the demand for unskilled labor has fallen in relative terms. This may well be the result of a shift in demand toward higher-quality products as per capita income has risen.[39] Or, perhaps more accurately, it has occurred as wealth has become more concentrated in many of these countries. What are required now are strategies to change the composition of demand for manufactured products and reverse this trend of the past three decades.

A key to any such strategy is greater income distribution, and integral to an approach of this kind is the combining of production and distribution in one process. More labor-intensive production means that many of the formerly unemployed would move into relatively low-paying, unskilled jobs. With increased purchasing power in the hands of the poor, the nature of consumer demand would become increasingly directed toward the traditional goods, which can be produced more labor-intensively. Hence, there would be a significant secondary employment effect. In effect, what would be achieved is the expansion of the domestic market, given the typical consumption patterns of the rich and the poor.

Of equal interest is the expansion of export markets, for this can also be an important source of job creation. Such expansion is not necessarily incompatible with labor-intensive production. Along this line, Walter Chudson observes that there has been a "... high rate of growth of exports of manufactures from certain developing countries in recent years. .... The bulk of such exports has been in relatively labor-intensive industries with stable technology compared with the 'high' technology of industrial countries."[40] A case can be made for focusing on the export of such traditional products as processed foods, textiles, leather, wood, and glass. With labor relatively cheap in Latin America, the labor-intensive industries of the region have some competitive advantage in the trade of their output. In addition, these industries presently have considerable idle capacity, which can be utilized.

At the same time, however, world demand is apparently shifting from the traditional goods of Latin America to the products of the more sophisticated industries. Furthermore, the protective barriers of the rich countries are highest against the importation of these traditional products. While there is hope for modest benefits from the new system of tariff preferences for the manufactures of the developing countries, these schemes are subject to serious limitations. Yet, though the greatest export potential may thus lie now with the dynamic industries of the continent, many of these industries can also be significantly more labor-intensive. Electronics, office machinery, motor vehicles, and transport equipment, among others, fall into this group,[41] further indicating the compatibility of less-mechanized production with expanded export markets.

THE CASE FOR LABOR-INTENSIVE TECHNOLOGIES

What is labor-intensive technology? Within the context of a full-employment industrial strategy, it comprises techniques and production processes that totally absorb those people desiring jobs, thereby increasing their participation in their economic environment. In the capitalist systems of Latin American industrial societies, it can be characterized more accurately as those processes that utilize the maximum number of workers while maintaining business profitability. To the extent that governments are willing and able to rectify distorted factor prices—specifically those of labor and capital—and even subsidize the use of labor for the social good, the definition of appropriate, labor-intensive technology changes to include more labor-utilizing techniques. And to the extent that companies take these new prices into account—recognizing their own engineering biases and the availability of more labor-intensive technologies (or the potential for their development)—the more frequently these processes will be utilized.

The degree of labor-intensivity can be measured in a variety of ways. The ILO uses the ratio of initial investment costs to the number of jobs created, and although there are some difficulties with this measure—including accurate definitions of capital and labor services[42]—it generally suffices. By using the number of workers rather than the total wage bill as a measure of labor involvement, it eliminates the possibility that an industry which utilizes a few skilled, highly paid workers could statistically appear to be labor-intensive.

Capital/labor ratios vary widely from industry to industry. In some, as much as $100,000 may be invested for the creation of one job, while in small, rural industries of Latin America, $1000 per worker is not an uncommon figure. Dr. E. F. Schumacher, founder of the London-based Intermediate Technology Development Group, suggests that modern technology begins at the $2500 per head level and fixes the level of intermediate technology (a term that describes labor-intensive but not primitive techniques) at about $250 per work place.[43] Another expert views this gap from a different perspective. According to Robin Clarke, in a labor-intensive economy it may take the equivalent of six months' salary to purchase the equipment required to provide work for one man, while the equivalent figure in a capital-intensive, advanced-technology economy is probably in the vicinity of 350 months' salary.[44]

The term *labor-intensive* is used here, rather than *intermediate* or *appropriate,* because it focuses attention upon the serious unemployment problems of Latin America. At the same time, "appropriate technology" as a broader term that not only emphasizes this large-scale unemployment but also other environmental ills,

... embraces a philosophy of development which is new, exciting and full of promise ... [These technologies] imply an attitude to industrialization so different from what has gone before ... they imply that the developing world need not—indeed should not—seek to copy the industrial pathways of the developed world. Such a conclusion today comes as something of a relief when the developed world is learning to its cost the heavy environmental price it has had to pay for its industrial development. And it perhaps spares us that lingering background fear that the world is heading for some awful crisis of uniformity and conformity. Appropriate technology means that industrial development can mean other things than smoking factory chimneys, oil pollution, social alienation and the worst effects of mass production. Instead, it can mean diversity, choice, craft industries, new and needed products and an alternative means of achieving the wealth that typifies the heavily industrialized nations.

The two essential ingredients to appropriate technology are local natural resources and cheap manpower. It is on these that the new industries for the developing world should be built up.[45]

The basis for industrial development in Latin America, however, has not been its labor resources. Industrial growth has meant, in fact, decreasing rates of labor absorption. This differs markedly from the industrial history of Western Europe.

In the previous century, the development of factory industry all over the world was inevitably accompanied by a substantial increase in factory employment. This happened in Western Europe, where factory industry came into being. Such is no longer the case. Industrial development in the less developed countries means in large measure the adaptation of advanced techniques. Up-to-date plants are being set up which are modelled on corresponding establishments in industrialized countries. Under these circumstances, the rapid growth of industrial production does not necessarily imply a substantial increase in industrial employment. With productivity growing quickly there is less need to increase employment. The rapid increase in factory productivity is practically a worldwide phenomenon today. In spite of the prevailing doubts as to whether the application of highly productive up-to-date techniques is economically warranted in the developing countries, where there is an enormous amount of disguised unemployment and wages are low, industrial development continues to be based primarily on the setting up and expansion of this type of establishment, no priority being attached to establishments based on more primitive techniques aimed at absorbing as much of the available labor force as possible.[46]

In today's industrialized countries, capital formation progressed simultaneously with the introduction of new production techniques, while in Latin America, ready-made techniques are being assimilated before sufficient capital has been accumulated. In addition, consumer demands are far more sophisticated in Latin America than they were in European countries at a similar stage of their development.[47] The result has been an increasing capital/labor ratio. The ILO found this to be true in Colombia, where the amount of fixed capital investment (measured in constant pesos) per new job more than doubled between the late 1950s and the mid-1960s.[48]

Three general arguments supporting this capital-intensive trend are offered here. (The availability of alternative technologies and the question of product quality will be discussed in Chapter III.) The first, quite simply, is that, although labor-intensive technologies may produce jobs in the short run, "it is far from certain that they lead to rapid development and thus to full employment in the long term."[49] The answer to that is the record of the past three decades. Unprecedented rates of industrial growth on the continent, with emphasis upon mechanization and modernization, have been paralleled by declining rates of labor absorption. In Colombia, for example, an average of nearly 11,000 new jobs were created annually between 1957 and 1961; during the following five years, the figure shrank to less than 7,000. Must we wait another thirty years when the problem is so immediate and pressing?[50]

The second argument falls under the general heading of conserving scarce resources. These resources include capital, raw materials, foreign exchange, trained labor (and labor training), and managerial or organizational skills. These skills, in turn, include planning, coordinating, scheduling, and production control.[51] Albert Hirshman focuses upon this last group:

Certain types of modern technology perform a crucial function in aiding management in the performance of new, unfamiliar, and perhaps somewhat uncongenial tasks. . . . Thus there are various ways in which capital enhances the efficiency of management and therefore of labor. This function of capital is of particular importance in underdeveloped societies where the tasks of coordination and of cooperation in large-scale organizations meet with special difficulties.[52]

In a 1955 publication, the Stanford Research Institute observed that ". . . an automatic machine may save so much of the time and cost that would otherwise be required for training labor and providing supervision, and may turn out so much more product, that this relatively heavier use of capital is justified, even in a country where the cost of capital is high."[53]

We need ask, however, so much more product than what? Is it more product per worker than through the use of labor-intensive techniques? If so, why is this desirable when millions of people in Latin America are looking for jobs? And why is there so much concern for conserving these particular "scarce" resources? What of those scarce resources that have been invested in the human capital of the continent in the form of education, literacy programs, health care, and birth control programs? These could be wasted, or at least their effects negated, if steady employment is not offered to these people. And within this context, the question must also be asked, development for whom? These poor and jobless are not just human capital, but human beings, and their education and medical care—and employment—are not merely contributions to the national product but, in today's world, unquestionably their due.

Despite these human considerations, special attention must still be paid to the risk of wasting scarce capital resources. It is argued that labor-intensive technologies not only lower the capital/labor ratio but also raise the ratio of capital to output. Although this is accepted without question in many circles, research conducted during the 1960s destroys this myth. Studies in the United Arab Republic, India, Taiwan, Japan, Chile, and Ecuador reveal that small firms, which generally had a much lower capital intensity than did large enterprises, achieved a higher productivity of capital than did their larger competitors in most industries.[54]

Finally, there is another argument, which is presented most clearly by Hirshman. He contends that it would be wasteful for a developing country

... to invest its scarce capital resources in duplicating lines of production that are already being carried on, even though inefficiently. A better use for capital would almost certainly be in the establishment of new-product industries. But in such industries capital-output ratios are likely to be typically high whereas they tend to be comparatively low in industries that would produce goods and services similar to those turned out by existing small-scale operators.[55]

There is total agreement here: capital-intensive competition with artisan work should be avoided whenever possible. On the other hand, why must new products necessarily be produced capital-intensively? This is best left unanswered until the range of technological choices is explored. But it should be stressed here that no "better use" of capital can be made than its distribution to the artisans and craftsmen of the region, who, unlike large companies, have no easy access to money at reasonable cost.

Numerous arguments can be made in favor of labor-intensive production in Latin America. They include the provision of more jobs from the same amount of capital; the existence of relatively cheap, abundant labor; the scarcity of capital and certain high labor skills; more equal income distribution; and the creation rather than displacement of traditional jobs. Other reasons have been offered, including the appropriateness of labor-intensive technologies for smaller-scale operations and smaller-sized markets. Taking all this into account, Everett Hagen concludes that in developing nations "the only machine methods that should be adopted are those which are technically impossible without the machines, plus those which can use a small amount of capital to substitute for an otherwise high labor cost."[56]

SUMMARY

Although an attack on unemployment must be a comprehensive one crossing sectoral lines, modern manufacturing, in particular, must make a greater contribution to the employment of Latin America's present jobless. This sector now accounts for one-quarter of the total output of the region and in the process of its growth has displaced artisan production and has generated large-scale migration to the cities. Capital-intensive production in the urban areas, however, has not created a sufficient number of jobs, either directly or indirectly. More labor-intensive manufacturing would have greater indirect employment effects and is compatible with both market expansion and changes in the product mix—two other means of providing new employment opportunities. Moreover, the hazards of following a labor-intensive approach have not been conclusively demonstrated. On the other hand, there are dangers in taking the capital-intensive road. "The premature introduction of advanced techniques may actually retard long-term growth," writes Jack Baranson,[57] citing the case of Soviet metal-fabricating industries of the 1930s. In our own day, the warning signals are even clearer. The United Nations World Plan states that during the 1960s, where capital-intensive technologies were transferred to developing countries, "widespread and increasing unemployment and underemployment, growing internal inequalities and social tensions" have been among the consequences.[58]

3 TECHNOLOGICAL CHOICE IN MANUFACTURING

If one accepts the arguments made heretofore on behalf of labor-intensive industrial production, there still remains the question of the availability of such techniques. There are many who claim that the urgent need for greater utilization of labor in the production process is not matched by a sufficiently broad choice on the technological shelf. In this view, labor-capital substitution is severely limited in the manufacturing sector. A contrasting view, however, is becoming increasingly accepted.

LABOR-INTENSIVE POSSIBILITIES

In a recent study, R. Hal Mason rejects real technical fixity as the main difficulty in labor intensivity and concludes, after drawing upon other sources, that "there is probably little doubt that the fixity of modern technology has been grossly exaggerated."[1] Sarah Jackson writes that, with the exception of only a few industries, "no one has yet been able to single out ... those industries for which there are not profitable alternative technologies."[2] And Hagen counters arguments which claim that there is a lack of labor-intensive processes by pointing out that "there are no verities of nature or of physics or chemistry that decree that less capital-intensive methods do not exist."[3]

As modern technologies evolved in the West, they were the product of the factors of the economic and social environment of those countries. Rising wages and the relative prices of labor and capital, in general, strongly influenced the degree of mechanization involved in production processes. It is not surprising, therefore, that in today's more modern (or dynamic) industries alternative technologies are more likely to be found lacking. Nor, using the same reasoning, is it strange that there is a greater range of technological choice within the more traditional industries of developing countries.

Scope within different manufacturing sectors. These two characterizations, traditional and modern, are the two most convenient categories for classifying manufacturing industries. They can also be grouped according to consumer goods, intermediate products, and capital (or investment) goods. This poses little problem, as the consumption goods and some of the intermediate products fall neatly into the traditional sector, while the rest of the intermediate and all of capital goods can be labeled modern.

In all, there are some twenty basic product groups. The traditional category includes clothing and footwear, food products, beverages, tobacco products, and furniture and furnishings—all consumer items; textiles, and leather goods, excluding shoes—considered either consumer or intermediate goods; rubber products, wood products, lumber and woodmaking, and perhaps cement—all intermediate products. The modern or dynamic category encompasses printing and publishing, paper and paper products, chemicals and petrochemicals, and petroleum and carbon derivatives—all intermediate industries; basic metals and nonmetallic mineral products—both either intermediate or capital; fabricated metal products, nonelectrical machinery, electrical machinery, and transportation equipment—all capital goods.

As implied earlier, traditional industries tend to be more labor-intensive than modern ones. Most of those placed in the traditional sector are often cited as having significant labor-intensive possibilities. Textiles, clothing, footwear, leather goods, furniture, rubber products, wood products, and woodmaking head the list, while the manufacture of toys can also absorb a great deal of labor. A controversy arises, however, in the important areas of food, drink, and tobacco. In a 1955 study, the Stanford Research Institute found that these industries had high capital requirements in most cases. Out of twenty industries rated in Australia in 1946-47, this same group was the eighteenth most labor-intensive. On the other hand, a similar ranking of U.S. industries in 1939 placed the group only eleventh,[4] indicating a probable flexibility of technological choice. Qualifications to asserted technological rigidity in food processing have been made, with reference to "some foodstuffs" and possible "marginal adjustments." The possibilities of using more labor in three types of food processing will be explored in depth later.

On the more dynamic side, electronic components, electrical equipment, and fabricated metal products can be produced rather labor-intensively. Electronics is often cited for this characteristic, while the other two ranked low in capital-intensivity on the Stanford chart. The ILO also found electrical machinery generally produced at a low level of mechanization as measured by horsepower per employee.[5] Bricks and tiles, which fall under the heading of nonmetallic mineral products, are claimed for both the labor- and capital-intensive columns. What all this indicates is that, in most cases, technological choice is not rigid and that instead we should be specifying those relatively few industries in which the scope for labor-capital substitution is small.

Pulp and paper, cement, and, as previously mentioned, food processing are seen as areas in which technology is relatively stabilized.[6] Otherwise, capital-intensive industries can be divided into two general categories: metal and oil processing and refining, on the one hand, and chemicals, on the other. This latter category includes petrochemicals and chemical fertilizer, as well. One proponent of labor-intensive technologies acknowledges that "there are obviously some basic heavy industries, such as steel and the chemical industry, where the most modern technology used in the West may still represent the best use of resources in the poor countries."[7]

In the smaller, poorer countries of Latin America, traditional goods manufacturing still predominates, but in most of the medium-sized and large nations, there has been a strong trend toward heavy industry. The result has been that the proportion of the region's industrial output held by food, beverages, tobacco, textiles, clothing, footwear, wood, and furniture has fallen 20 percent from the over 60 percent share it had two decades ago, while the modern industries have gained a significantly greater proportion. The latter includes chemicals and petroleum products (16.7 percent of regional production in 1968) and the basic metals (6.6 percent), principally iron and steel; the most dynamic growth of all, however, has come in the area of metal transforming, in which there are real labor-intensive possibilities. This sector—which is understood to include fabricated metal products, electrical and nonelectrical equipment, and transportation equipment— more than doubled its share of industrial output during the 1950s and constituted over one-fifth of regional industrial production by 1968.[8]

This trend should continue and could spread through the region if Colombia provides an accurate indication. Consumer goods represented two-thirds of modern industrial output there in 1967, but their production was growing relatively slowly. While increased demand, both domestic and foreign, could accelerate this growth, it is in the newly emerging intermediate and capital goods industries where the real dynamism is to be found. The emphasis in this sector, however, has been placed upon machinery production—rather than upon the more rigidly capital-intensive chemicals and metal processing groups—because the possibilities for import substitution in this area are considered to be very great.[9]

A key to determining which industries have the greatest labor-absorbing potential may be the production stage around which the industry is centered. The major division is made between industries principally involved with process-centered operations and those concerned with product-centered operations. The continuous-process industries, which include chemicals, petrochemicals, metal refining, oil refining, and brewing, appear to have rather limited scope for capital displacement within the production process itself.[10] According to Baranson, a "distinguishing characteristic of processing industries such as steel and oil refining is that they are almost necessarily capital-intensive and machine-paced even at a small scale." The line is drawn between processing plants and the manufacturing and assembly industries (e.g., automotive, mechanical, and electrical equipment) "which involve . . . the efficient integration of thousands of steps to machine and finish hundreds of different parts for final assembly."[11]

A recent study by Jan F. van Houten of the International Monetary Fund analyzes the assembly industries in the Caribbean and establishes the labor-intensive nature of those operations. In Jamaica, for example, of the 192 firms receiving economic incentives from the government in 1970, only 12 percent involved assembly—but they employed a full 35 percent of the workers. A year later, the employment figure was up a percent, although the assembly plants accounted for only 11 percent of the value of total production under the incentive laws. Elsewhere, in Barbados and in Port-au-Prince, Haiti, about 20 percent of manufacturing employment is generated in assembly industries.[12]

It is on the subject of labor absorption in raw material processing vis-à-vis more product-oriented endeavors that two authorities in the field are in apparent conflict. Gustav Ranis recently wrote the following:

One tentative conclusion which may be derived from these plant visits is that the closer the production process is to the raw material processing stage, that is, backward linkages, the smaller the chances for efficient labor/capital substitution statically or capital-stretching innovations dynamically; the closer the process to the finished product stage, the greater are these possibilities.[13]

Yet Baranson specifically points to materials processing as an area in which "plant engineering and equipment design can yield higher levels of economic employment. . . ."[14] He also indicates the advantage of carrying on these activities in the rural areas:

Among the various benefits of interaction between agriculture and rural-based industry are the increasing possibilities for the use of labor-intensive industrial technology. Rural-based industry is more likely to incorporate indigenous technological change or the rearrangement of factors along new types of labor-using production functions.[15]

This view is also held by others who see the greatest labor-intensive potential in food processing, textiles, and other rural industries.[16]

Rather than a direct conflict, however, these differing points of view appear to indicate that there exists a wide range of industries in which technological flexibility allows for greater labor substitution. While it is acknowledged that there are a few process-centered operations—most particularly the chemicals and metal processing groups—in which capital displacement possibilities are quite limited, the potential in other areas may be much greater.

Central production processes. "A process-centered industry," according to Hirshman, "will typically contain a *central* mechanical or chemical process which takes place in a series of machine-controlled operations."[17] It is around such a basic process that factory work often "falls into place almost naturally...." Hagen contends that some factor substitution is possible within many of these central processes, but acknowledges that there are some cases in which a method to reduce capital requirements presently does not exist.[18]

This is quite different from arguing that labor substitution is not possible because it reduces plant efficiency and coordination. Hirshman sees these as major attributes of modern technology which have their greatest impact in process-centered rather than product-centered industries. Efficiency is maintained as long as the central process sets the pace of all operations in the plant.[19] What must be made clear, however, is that this argument concerns efficiency and not technological rigidity. The labor substitution issue then boils down, in good part, to a trade-off between labor productivity and employment, as well as to questions of product quality and raw materials and inventory costs.

Machine-paced operations are typically more capital-intensive than operator-paced ones in the sense that investment in machinery will raise the ratio between capital investment and the total wage bill. On the other hand, such operations can allow for the substitution of many low-paid, unskilled workers for a few highly paid, skilled ones—thus maintaining or even lowering the capital/labor ratio in the most relevant sense, that is, the number of jobs created per unit of capital invested. Hirshman claims that machine-paced operations tend to employ labor more efficiently than do operator-paced processes, which permit a wide scope for poor performance. He explains that an untrained labor force has a greater chance of performing better in machine-paced operations "not so much because of a tendency toward slacking when the machine does not compel the work, as because machine-paced operations provide for steadiness of pace and regular brief rest periods which the inexperienced self-paced worker has difficulty in observing."[20]

Operator-paced activities, in which the operator can work at his own speed, can be divided into two types—routine operations and dexterity operations. Latin American workers have been observed as being well-suited for routine work—janitors, guards, floor boys, hand truckers, material handling laborers, packers—but not for dexterity operations.[21] This is a curious finding. On the one hand, the statement that these people would have more trouble with dexterous work than with routine or machine-paced tasks is applicable to other cultures, as well. On the other, Latins—both women and men—appear to have considerable aptitude for this type of work, certainly for using a sewing machine and cutting materials. As for such activities as mixing chemicals and batches of materials, they require good training and supervision as much as they do dexterity. In fact, in Puerto Rico, where the culture is quite similar to that of Latin America, the greatest success has been achieved in those industries containing highly standardized and repetitive operations for which manual dexterity is the main requirement. The most difficulty has been encountered in areas in which workers are left with considerable discretion and require greater supervision.[22]

Quality and cost considerations. The most important question arising from this analysis involves the relationship between labor efficiency in these operations and the quality of the product, for what we are concerned with here is the ability to produce—in a more labor-intensive fashion—basically the same end product. Baranson argues that "quality and precision requirements place absolute limits on the technical feasibility of substituting human skills for machine capabilities." Precision and uniformity are built into automated equipment, particularly in high-volume production.[23]

On the other hand, however, capital-intensive production is often not covered well by present control systems and, when dealing in large volumes, a single error can be quite costly. In addition, product quality standards are not always strict, and in many instances, engineering and consumer standards are not necessarily the same. Furthermore, a study of some light manufacturing operations in Indonesia revealed that, although the *most* labor-intensive techniques available generally produced inferior products— at least by engineering standards—intermediate technologies yielded products that were comparable in quality to those of advanced techniques.[24] Many of the participants at a 1970 United Nations conference in Medellín, Colombia, raised the issue of employing labor-intensive technology to produce a high-quality product at competitive costs and, in response, it was suggested that such intermediate technology could be patterned on techniques available in some smaller European countries.[25]

Cost and price considerations are often more important to the market position of a firm than is product quality. In those cases, plant efficiency is of particular importance; but a decision on the choice of production techniques should not be made without attention first being given to relative factor prices. In addition, it should be kept in mind when selecting a technique that it is not only labor-intensive operations that suffer inefficiencies. Latin American industries which use the same technology as that in use in the United States and Europe have been found at times to operate less efficiently and with higher costs than their counterparts in developed countries.[26] As concerns inventory costs, labor-intensive methods may raise these by increasing the length of the product cycle,[27] but as for the saving of raw materials, this may be an overrated reason for choosing capital-intensive technologies.[28]

Ancillary operations. Although expanded employment possibilities appear to be limited in many process-centered operations, substantial numbers of new jobs can be created in these manufacturing industries in other ways. They include greater labor substitution in ancillary operations, reduction of the scale of production, and the utilization of multiple shifts.

Process-centered industries do not necessarily consist entirely of machine-paced operations.[29] Movements toward and away from that process can be man-paced. In the pre-processing stage, workers can substitute for machines in handling material inputs and can do the same in post-process packaging and in the outward movement of the final product. It is a matter of seeking out those operations in which the substitution is feasible. Of the many activities ancillary to the basic process that can be done manually rather than mechanically, Mason lists some of the more obvious. They include "materials handling; preparation of parts; packing, filling, and packaging; grading and inspection; painting and finishing; manual transfer between production line segments; and inventorying and order picking."[30] Storage and the transfer of supplies into and out of warehouses can be added to the list, as can the increased maintenance required by the use of older equipment. In total, these activities often constitute a large part of the production operations of an enterprise.

The Japanese demonstrated the possibility of greater labor absorption in in-plant transportation by devising human conveyor belts. They now use a mechanical conveyor belt system, but the Koreans have followed their earlier example and Mason has noted that in Mexico (as well as in the Philippines), mechanical conveyors are not used much in the assembly of transport equipment. The Japanese also used to do most of their packaging by hand. A recent look at the bottling and packing of pills in Mexico and Puerto Rico revealed that bottle filling tends to be done semiautomatically, while the final carton packing—a step involving a lower volume of discrete units—is done manually.[31] A few years ago, an American firm in Brazil considered doing its packaging and bottling in the Northeast, principally to benefit from tax incentives. The plant would have been labor-intensive, employing unskilled labor and providing some training, because there would have been too many different procedures to automate. The decision not to implement the plan had nothing to do with technical feasibility, but rather was the result of the poor quality of supplies, as well as limited demand in the area.

Scale of production. A reduction in the scale of production can also contribute to capital-stretching and hence to employment. Smaller-sized plants are generally less capital-intensive (though not necessarily so). In any event, even if it is difficult to employ more people per unit of output in the key production phase, more employment can be generated in the ancillary operations through scaling down. There is a proportional increase in the need for, among other things, material handling and assembly, the preparation of raw materials, and the distribution of the final product.

Market demand is the most important factor in determining the appropriate scale of production for many industries. Domestic demand is rather small in many countries of Latin America because of relatively small national populations and extreme inequities in income distribution. Plant size requirements may well be as little as one-tenth the optimum according to world standards. It is not uncommon that the break-even production level of a mechanized plant is found to be too high for the home market. Unfortunately in such cases the answer has typically been (where export possibilities have been limited) to give protection to the industry rather than to attempt to substitute more labor for the machines. Relatively low labor costs help maintain the competitiveness of small-scale operations, as do the savings on the distribution of the output to smaller, more localized markets.

Market size, however, is not the only important consideration. "For some processes," writes Robert P. Morgan of Washington University in St. Louis, "it may be that economies of scale dominate the situation. In those cases, smaller plants will be uneconomical and noncompetitive. On the other hand, there may be other processes in which smaller plants can do reasonably well, particularly if designed to take advantage of lower labor costs."[32] Textiles, clothing, toys, radios, and furniture are some of the products that have been found not to suffer from diseconomies of small-scale production. The food industry is also cited. Not only can a satisfactory level of efficiency be attained but, if labor costs are substantially low, the export competitiveness of these goods may even be improved.[33]

In scaled-down textile production, the inputs are cheap raw materials, simple equipment, and large numbers of workers. Such enterprises compete side by side with large, modern establishments in Latin America.[34] Likewise, the Philips Company of the Netherlands has demonstrated that a radio assembly plant can be designed for small-volume, low-cost production utilizing unskilled workers.[35] A United Nations study reveals that in some industrial groups in Latin America

... productivity remains constant or even diminishes as the size of the enterprise increases. This applies, for instance, to textiles; footwear and other wearing apparel; wood and cork; furniture and fixtures; leather and leather products; and transport equipment. Even in the United States, the productivity ... [in the manufacture of] textiles, footwear, and other wearing apparel decreases from over $5,700 per person for enterprises with 5 to 9 employees to little more than $4,000 for those with 50 or more employees.[36]

For small-scale production, intermediate technology (in terms of scale and industrial sophistication) is required to avoid excess capacity. A case has been cited in which there had been two alternative ways of making an import-substitution investment:

The market for the product had previously amounted to 25,000 units, supplied by imports. One alternative, which had called for an investment of $5 million, had implied the employment of forty-five workers and a capacity well in excess of the local demand. The second alternative, using intermediate technology, less automation and much more labour, and producing an identical product, had called for an investment of $800,000 in a plant employing 100 workers. The second plan had been chosen. The firm's product, marketed under an internationally licensed brand name, had captured 90 percent of the market, which had grown to 40,000 units in one year.[37]

The fact that the firm eventually increased plant mechanization as the volume of output grew detracts neither from the original decision to produce labor-intensively nor from the efficiency of the equipment originally in use. Such appropriate technology generally incorporates machines that have smaller capacities and are more flexible (i.e., less specialized or single-purpose) as well as more processes of a batch nature rather than of a continuous type. Sometimes, however, the smallest capacity of the equipment—packaging and labeling machinery are good examples—is still too large for the task at hand.[38]

Smaller-scale production may not be an effective means for increasing labor absorption in all industries. Continuous-process industries involving mixing, flowing, cooking, filtering, and chemical-type processes in general remain rather capital-intensive in small-scale production and can suffer from diseconomies at that level of output.[39] The costs of production of such things as electronics, automotive products, and metal working are also sensitive to the diseconomies of small-scale operations, and maintaining quality control and material standards can pose difficult problems.[40] The automotive industry in Latin America has been particularly troublesome in this respect, as countries have insisted upon having their own national industry. But these difficulties do not necessarily preclude the use of relatively less capital-intensive techniques in larger-scale production than is often currently the case in the production of many of these goods.

Export competitiveness. Before discussing the use of multiple shifts to increase the numbers employed in the factories of the continent, it is appropriate at this point to raise the question of export competitiveness. As has been referred to earlier, doubts have been expressed as to the competitive cost and quality of the output produced in a more labor-intensive manner and/or at a reduced scale of production in many, if not most, industries. There is also a school of thought that holds just the opposite.

Ranis belongs to this second group. He argues that ". . . the typical developing country, especially one which is open and not too large in size, can expect—with appropriate policy changes taking place—to transit from import substitution, with pure technological transplantation the order of the day, to export substitution, with labor-using innovations taking on major significance."[41] In this view, the economy shifts to a "human-resource-based system" in the export substitution phase. According to Louis T. Wells' product life cycle theory,[42] products themselves also evolve to a mature state at which, in developing countries, they are most suitable for export. Technological stability and a greater use of unskilled labor usually marks this stage. Baranson adds that "exports of labor-intensive manufacturers can be an important contributor to growth at transitional stages of development."[43]

The ILO notes in its Colombian study that, in many countries, the processing of rural products is one of the cheapest and most efficient ways of increasing employment and stimulating agricultural production and stresses the importance of export markets in this area. Although the study emphasizes the need to maintain product quality, its focus is not on the production process, but rather on problems of product preservation and even more so on the farms themselves and their linkages with the factories.[44]

Of course, it can be argued—and often is—that quality control is best maintained through the use of modern processing machinery. Product standardization and low unit costs are among the essentials for export competitiveness and, according to this argument, can best be assured in capital-intensive production. It appears that a closer item-by-item examination of the food industry must be made to determine the possibilities of labor-capital substitution and the effects upon quality and cost.

On the other hand. the clothing and footwear industries more clearly combine labor intensivity and export potential. For example, some of the best shoes Bata produces for the European market are produced in a rather labor-intensive fashion. Another firm, engaged in the manufacture of a specific line of clothing in Mexico, did not adopt labor-intensive production techniques until it moved primarily into exporting. It then found that by substituting more labor it could more than double its 10 percent profit margin while producing a product of identical quality. Previously, the company had not bothered to alter its more mechanized facilities, as import substitution production had already yielded large profits.

While traditional goods still have good export potential, they are currently being surpassed in many instances by the more dynamic industries of the continent. But, as was indicated earlier, not all these products have to be produced capital-intensively in order to be competitive. Electronic components and parts head a group of goods—including motor vehicles (particularly buses), transport equipment, many types of machinery, and machine tools—that has been moving up on export lists and that can be efficiently produced with a relatively large labor input. The future of at least some of these industries could depend upon the use of fairly simple production systems and large amounts of unskilled labor.

Multiple shifts. Finally, an effective way of increasing manufacturing employment without increasing capital costs and without altering the production function itself is the use of two or three daily shifts. This could be extremely useful to many industries, as would the use of more labor per machine at any given time to eliminate idle machine time. Multiple shifts were part of the Japanese development program, which was designed in part to overcome capital scarcity.

W. Paul Strassmann points to the drawbacks of this method of capital stretching. They include higher wages to night-shift workers, the difficulties surrounding night-shift breakdowns, and the greater flexibility of a one-shift plant.[45] He and others also emphasize the scarcity of technicians and managers, which limits the number of shifts that workers are able to work under expert supervision.

The major obstacles to the greater use of multiple shifts in Latin

America, however, are institutional. One of these is the institution of overtime, which is well established throughout the region. The ILO study found in 1969 that over 60 percent of the occupied population of Bogotá worked 48 or more hours per week and that the trend toward more overtime work was probably growing.[46] In Costa Rica, it has been suggested that labor laws be changed to allow two or three shifts instead of overtime by existing personnel.[47] Labor laws throughout most of the region have proven to be a roadblock. For example, the two main provisions that have discouraged shift work in Colombia have been the requirements that workers be paid 35 percent more between 6 P.M. and 6 A.M. and the prohibition of work by women between 10 P.M. and 5 A.M. The latter restriction—which is common throughout most of Latin America—has been particularly detrimental to the textile and clothing industries.[48]

A SURVEY OF SELECTED INDUSTRIES

While it is important to identify the capital-stretching and labor-absorbing techniques available in the manufacturing sector as a whole, what is most necessary today is an industry-by-industry analysis of labor-intensive potentialities. Accordingly, there follows an examination of some twenty industries in varying degrees of depth—most of which make significant contributions to Latin American economies.

The *textile industry* is usually one of the first to be established during the process of industrialization. It has been of considerable importance to developing countries with regard to employment creation, as it has historically been labor-intensive in nature. Technological advancements during the past two decades have transformed textiles into a potentially highly capital-intensive industry, however, and the trend continues in that direction. But the option not to adopt the most modern technology is open to developing countries, which ". . . have a wider range of machinery than in perhaps any other industry to suit the particular ratio of capital to labour cost, the availability of skills and the size of the market."[49] Technical obsolescence in the more developed countries has helped create a large reservoir of used textile machinery.

Modern textile equipment essentially consists of a basic machine unit and various devices that control quality or move material on or off the machine. It is in the selection of these devices, many of which are optional, that the degree of automation can be determined. Automatic devices can sometimes be justified on the grounds of significant improvement in product quality, but more often than not it cannot be justified in a labor-abundant country.

Another approach to increased labor use in the division of the spinning and weaving processes into separate industries, as there exists less scope for using labor-intensive methods for the former than for the latter. Yarn could be spun at a large capital-intensive mill, which would supply several small labor-intensive weaving mills or even rural homes where the cloth would be woven. In the case of some specialist yarns, several small spinning mills have supplied a single weaving mill, suggesting that the possibilities for small-scale, labor-intensive production in both processes should be explored further. It has already been found that unit production and investment costs for a spinning mill with as few as 6,000 spindles are only marginally higher than those for a mill with 100,000 spindles.[50] As for the weaving process, substantial savings can be made on plant expenditures—the major capital cost—through the use of looms in numerous small plants. Small mills are labor-intensive in and of themselves and, in addition, increased manpower is required for the additional transport and handling involved.[51]

Textile manufacturing does not require a highly skilled labor force. In fact, even in a modern integrated mill less than one-quarter of the workers need be skilled. Semiskilled labor is most in demand and the necessary training is not very extensive, although that of weavers and loom fixers is of relatively longer duration.[52] The work force in the textile industries of two major Latin American producers, Colombia and Mexico, is today dominated by men. Despite the past practice of employing unskilled, low-wage women laborers, the importation of modern machinery and the general trend toward capital intensivity has given rise to the substitution of what is perceived as a more productive male work force.[53]

At the turn of the century in Japan, on the other hand, there was a clear desire not to employ the day's modern textile technology before the development of a skilled labor force and entrepreneurial capabilities. Second-hand machinery was imported from England and, particularly in the weaving process, nonautomatic techniques were chosen from a rather wide range of alternatives. In addition, seven workers were used per machine, as compared to three in England, with the extra people binding broken threads and maintaining the older equipment. A final method of capital stretching employed was the use of multiple, or at least double, shifts, which permitted the spinning mills to run twenty-two hours a day and the cotton weaving to be done twenty hours daily.[54]

After a half century or more of technological stagnation in the textile industry, dramatic changes have been made since about 1950. An ECLA study reveals the increasing capital intensivity of integrated cotton mills in Latin America between 1950 and 1965. Capital investment for a typical mill rose almost 50 percent during that period, while output increased less than 30 percent and, most significantly, the rate of labor absorption more than halved.[55] This slow absorption rate throughout the region was most dramatically demonstrated in Argentina, Brazil, and Chile, where the total amount of labor employed actually declined. The most important factor in this phenomenon was the adoption of more capital-intensive production techniques.[56]

There is good reason, in light of the prevailing factor prices, to doubt the rationality of some of the investment decisions that contributed to this trend. In the early 1950s, for example, the ratio between the hourly cost of running textile machinery and the price of a man-hour was five times greater in Chile than in the United States.[57] Lower wage levels can be offset by very low worker productivity, as has been cited by ECLA in a 1963 study of the Brazilian textile industry.[58] Any reference, however, to a relatively high labor cost per unit of fabric is rather meaningless without knowledge of the degree of capital intensivity. Even in Colombia, where the manual dexterity of the workers is generally excellent and labor productivity is the highest on the continent, many mills, particularly the larger ones, are now capital-intensive. This is so in spite of the fact that those involved in textile manufacturing in Colombia believe labor-intensively produced textiles can compete in foreign markets.

The sales emphasis in Latin American textiles has been rapidly shifting from the domestic market to exporting, with export incentives offered in most countries. Although the textile market is generally protected in the region, the opportunity for further import substitution is small. If an export trade to developed countries is to be established, the fabrics offered must be at least partially made from man-made fibers. In this regard, Latin America is fortunate that it is well advanced in the manufacture of synthetics.[59] Foreign firms have made a sizable contribution in the area, although some U. S. companies are still in cotton textiles with a highly diversified product mix. Regardless of the fibers used, the main advantage these countries have in export competition is a relatively low wage level—another reason for the use of labor-intensive production processes.

At the other end of the scale is the *chemical industry,* in which the scope for labor substitution in the production process is considerably more limited. It generally provides very few unskilled jobs and relatively few opportunities for skilled workers, while requiring a relatively high number of technical and professional personnel. This is to be expected, given that these industries were developed in high-wage countries. Possibilities for labor-capital substitution are further limited by the fact that the manufacture of chemical products is a continuous-process rather than mechanical-transforming operation and thus offers fewer choices of alternative processes.[60]

In a report prepared during the summer of 1972 at the Universidad Nacional Autónoma de Mexico,[61] appropriate technologies for the industry were considered for developing countries. One of the first conclusions presented in the study is that the chemical industry consists of a number of subsectors, which have varying abilities to absorb labor without causing considerable inefficiencies. The petrochemical and petroleum refining sectors, for instance, were found to involve large-scale, capital-intensive technologies, and their products could not be produced at a much smaller scale or more labor-intensively without becoming uncompetitive. On the other hand, plastics conversion can be carried out efficiently at smaller production levels and with greater labor utilization.

Considered as a whole, the chemical industry today has a base technology that is by nature and necessity capital-intensive. The Mexican study, however, traces the evolution of the industry in the developed countries and argues that commercial processes were developed and subsequent modifications made in an economic environment that called for economies of scale and a greater use of capital vis-à-vis labor. This indicates that there may well have been discarded along the way smaller-scale and more labor-intensive technological alternatives. The choice of an appropriate technology for a developing economy with small markets and unemployment problems should therefore extend beyond the current alternatives to include those that were considered but not implemented years ago.

Perhaps more importantly, consideration should be given to the modification of existing technology. The study identifies three areas of possible chemical process modifications. The first involves changes in operations, that is, primarily a change from dilute, continuous processing to batch, semicontinuous processing using concentrated liquids. Batch processing greatly facilitates efficient small-scale production, which is a central concern in the adaptation process. To quote the report: "That such an adaptation process [to smaller-scale production] can, in certain circumstances, be carried out successfully is generally accepted by process engineers.... However, it should be kept in mind that successful adaptation experience is not necessarily universal, nor even widespread."[62]

The second change involves the scaling-down of chemical plants and the elimination of excess equipment, which small-size batch processing would allow. Although other sources claim that scaled-down chemical plants are not any less capital-intensive than larger ones,[63] the Mexican study's finding that the capital/labor ratio may be reduced in such circumstances is supported by research conducted in the 1960s. A United Nations study found that labor inputs in the chemical industry are strongly subject to economies of scale. "The correlation of labour inputs with the scale of output," the report reads, "indicates an elasticity of the order of 0.2; thus even large increases in scale will produce only small additional labour requirements...."[64] Conversely, a few smaller chemical plants would employ substantially more labor than one large one. In these smaller factories the focus would be upon avoiding the use of excessive design factors and unnecessary large equipment and upon the substitution of labor where possible. Materials handling, as well as other ancillary operations, is an activity that can be much more labor-intensive, although it has been estimated that the maximum capital savings achievable in this manner is only about 5 to 10 percent.[65]

Changes in the control system is a third area for examination and it has been shown that here, too, smaller-scale operations can permit greater labor-intensivity. The report explains:

Processes developed in industrialized countries are using to a great extent very sophisticated computerized control systems to reduce the use of labor and to prevent a disaster condition that would arise because of the large production flaws, in case of any failure in the process. When these processes are adapted to a smaller scale of operation, it is possible to replace some of these automatic control systems by manual controls, because labor is generally less expensive and the risk of accident in case of a process failure diminishes with the plant capacity.[66]

There are other ways of increasing labor utilization, including increasing the number of workers per machine. This can be accomplished either by reducing the operating speed of the equipment or by using multiple worker shifts. But all in all, the chemical industry does not lend itself to much labor absorption and few modifications have been made to suit local requirements. Petrochemical plants, in particular, are largely standardized and have seen only minor adaptations. Petrochemical companies, as well as other chemical manufacturers, look for large markets, which can support production facilities using economies of scale and sophisticated machinery. Brazil is now such a market and an ideal base for Latin American production by foreign firms.

In a related field, the *pharmaceutical industry,* the potential use of labor-intensive methods is much greater. The manufacturing process consists basically of tableting and packaging, both of which can be done manually. Although it has been observed that these activities are already performed in a highly labor-intensive manner in Latin America, it was found that in Mexico the process of stamping chemical grains into pills is likely to be wholly automatic.[67] This is particularly true of high-volume production. There is reason to believe that successful regional integration in Latin America, by expanding otherwise small, protected domestic markets, would allow and lead to both specialization and greater labor-intensivity in pharmaceutical production.

A difficult industry to classify in terms of its labor-absorption potential is *food processing.* Some authorities suggest that modern, mechanized processing facilities are generally required, particularly in order to assure high and uniform quality standards for competition in world markets.[68] There do appear to be exceptions to this rule, however, both as concerns the types of produce processed and some aspects of quality control. According to people in the industry, for example, impurities are generally not a problem in labor-intensive processes and even products like mayonnaise, which are prone to spoiling, can be hand-packed without loss of quality. What, in fact, may contribute most to capital-intensivity in many instances is the size of the market. There is evidence that a firm will enter a small market with a low level of technology and, as the market expands, the equipment will become more sophisticated.

Corn processing, an important activity in Latin American economies, is a case in point. While fairly sophisticated control devices are necessary, the degree of plant mechanization is determined principally by the size of the operation. This requires one qualification. The modern, capital-intensive, wet-starch process does produce a purer product in the sense that proteins and other solubles are removed and the product is given a higher-quality appearance. The advantage then of the older technologies is not only that they call for a greater use of labor but that important proteins are preserved for the poor of the region, who might otherwise not receive them.

Economies of scale are emphasized, however, as the major reason for increasing the degree of mechanization. The smallest operation possible using modern techniques is 150 tons of corn grinding a day. As volume rises, costs go down, because manpower requirements level off at a certain level of output. A firm operating in two Latin American countries—one small, the other relatively large—uses labor-intensive methods in the former and the most efficient and mechanized techniques in the latter. Although daily output is forty times greater for the larger market, only little more than double the number of workers are employed on the factory floor. Interestingly enough, it is the packaging stage—which absorbs two-thirds of the workers in the smaller plant—rather than the processing stage itself that suffers the greatest labor displacement in the larger-scale production. The number of packers actually decreases absolutely despite the manifold increase in output.

This demonstrates a quite significant fact: that the food processing industry can be a major labor absorber even if the processing itself is done capital-intensively for reasons of efficiency and product quality. It is in packaging that the greatest use of unskilled workers can be made. Yet as the total labor costs in this operation rise along with the volume of production, machines usually replace the workers. If, in the preceding illustration, the number of workers engaged in packaging had increased proportionately with the growth in output, sixty times the number of people would have had jobs. Thus the scale of operation, the choice of technology, and the degree of packaging mechanization are all important considerations in this industry in relation to its job-creating potential.

Similar conclusions can be made about other food-processing industries. In his study of African *sugar-processing* factories, James Pickett discovered that both the labor-intensive, Khandsari-type, open-pan, sulphitation process and the "modern" vacuum pan process were capable of producing a high-quality, mill-white product. As is the case with corn products in developing countries, he also found that there exists a segmented market for sugar:

Demand for this [high-quality] product comes from fussy consumers. Less fussy consumers, bakers and confectioners (for example) would settle for a product of lower quality and lower price. No sensible relaxation of the in-built quality controls of the modern mill-white vacuum pan process could cater for this diversified demand. As it happens, the open-pan process normally yields several grades of sugar in a course of a production cycle.[69]

It was also found that, under local economic conditions, the Khandsari-type process was both privately more profitable, because it used considerably less capital, and socially more beneficial, in that it employed significantly more full-time, and substantially more seasonal, workers.[70]

Ancillary operations are emphasized by Howard Pack as the prime employment generators in his look at the *fruit-processing* industry in Kenya. He asserts that only a small percentage of the labor force is involved in the central processing operation.

Thus in a large fruit processing plant employing over one hundred workers, the actual processing of jam or the cooking of other fruits is done in a vat into which three workers pour ingredients which have been mixed by hand. A more advanced process would involve automatic weighing of the ingredients and filling of the vat. Nevertheless, the three represent a small fraction of the total force and if they were replaced by automatic vat filling equipment requiring one person to flip dials, total plant employment would decline by only two workers.[71]

The bulk of the workers would still be employed in the four other basic processes identified by Pack—material receiving, material handling among processes, packaging, and storage of the finished product.

He also analyzes *paint production* in the same fashion and concludes that there, too, most employment occurs in ancillary activities. In Kenyan plants, drums are unloaded by hand and kept in the factory, as opposed to

British plants, which have automatic receiving lines. Likewise, there is virtually no use of mechanical conveyors for intrafactory material movements. Although automated filling is one of the simplest processes to introduce, small batch size and the consequent certainty of excess capacity have also ruled against its introduction. The primarily manual operation used instead may involve a half dozen or more steps ranging from hand ladling to manual weighing and weight correction of the filled bags, and can thereby generate major amounts of employment. The storage process is also a major employer of labor (usually about 20 percent of the plant work force), as low wage rates dictate against the substitution of fork-lift trucks.[72]

In another processing industry—*tobacco*—the range of technological options is wide. The primary processing stage—cleaning, packing, and aging—can be rather labor-intensive. In cigarette manufacturing, the choice of an intermediate technology, which includes some hand preparation of the tobacco, can mean employment of twice as many workers than in a totally mechanized process. Employment rises are even more striking when the cigarettes are hand-rolled and the tobacco is primarily hand-prepared.[73] Unfortunately, cigar manufacturing is going the other route in the Brazilian state of Bahia. Piecework cigar production is being replaced by more capital-intensive methods as wages rise and mass-production techniques are introduced.[74]

Rubber products include a wide range of items, but in general it can be said that this can be a relatively labor-intensive industry. There are products, like hose and belting, which require close control of the manufacturing process, highly skilled labor, and heavy equipment, but a host of household items, along with canvas and rubber footwear, demand a good deal of manual work. Tires can also be made in a variety of ways, some significantly more labor-intensive than others.[75]

The most revealing study conducted in this area was an examination by the ILO in the mid-1960s of the rubber products industries of five Asian nations. Investment per worker in the Philippines was found to be 50 percent higher than in Japan and about four times greater than in Taiwan and Korea. An explanation is provided by James Grant of the Overseas Development Council:

. . . in the Philippines, because machinery was subsidized and import substitution heavily protected it has been profitable until recently to import Western technologies wholesale. In Japan, on the other hand, where machinery is more expensive than in the West because capital is scarcer and where the more abundant labor is cheaper, the technologies have been adapted to that situation. . . . The rubber products produced in Korea and Taiwan appear to be just as good and just as profitable as those made in India and they provide nearly twice as much employment for a given amount of investment in the industry.[76]

It is clear that technological feasibility, quality control, and production efficiency are not roadblocks in the way of labor-intensive production of these products.

Plastic products, on the other hand, do not usually require much labor in relation to the value of output. In fact, one of the main reasons for the success of plastics in developed countries has been the ease with which large numbers of identical units can be produced with less labor than would be required using other materials such as wood, metal, ceramics, or shell. The industry, however, is not totally without a labor-intensive potential. In molding processes, for example, automatic machines can be replaced by hand-operated and hand-controlled machinery and much additional manpower.[77] In the manufacture of a particular product—plastic sandals—it has been shown that the use of semiautomatic, rather than wholly automatic, injectors can mean a fourfold increase in the number of workers employed.[78]

The *shoe-manufacturing industry* itself offers a wide range of production techniques. From existing operations conventionally used in Africa and the United Kingdom, Pickett identifies three basic processes, which we can call modern, intermediate, and labor-intensive. The first requires cutting the upper to shape on power presses, machine lasting, and other mechanized operations. The second calls for hand-cutting of upper leather and machine-aided hand-lasting. The third involves hand-cutting of uppers, hand-lasting, and the minimum of other machine operations consistent with the production of shoes of comparable quality to that produced in the more mechanized factories. It was found in Ghana and Ethiopia that use of such a labor-intensive process would triple the labor/capital ratio of modern factories, increase employment in the vicinity of 30 percent, and also lead to greater private profitability.[79] As such private returns may not be realized elsewhere under different economic conditions, some intermediate technologies could be introduced. For example, it is quicker to stitch the sole to the upper and insole with simple Blake sewing machines than by hand, and these machines may be more appropriate than vulcanizing or injection-molding soling equipment.[80]

Can manufacturing is an industry for which highly automatic, semiautomatic, and nonautomatic equipment are available. In the sealing operation, the most sophisticated technique—which calls for very little manual effort—involves the use of heavy machinery capable of sealing four cans at a time. Reforming and assembly require only two workers per can line, with the need eliminated for additional personnel to move materials between machines and for storage. In capital-intensive packaging operations, cans are automatically installed on a wide conveyor belt and then dropped row by row into cartons. All things considered, an automatic can line in this industry may be a necessity at times, particularly when large volume output and precision work are required.

A semiautomatic sealing process uses small machines, which seal one can at a time and require one operator per machine. His job is to load the machine with a can cylinder, swing a lever, and then place the sealed can on a conveyor belt. Quality control is a minor problem, in that a skilled supervisor must be employed for every three or four machines and the record shows that usually 5 percent of final output does not meet international standards. Labor-intensive packaging methods involve a worker using a wooden device to pick up a whole row of cans and drop it into a carton. The advantage of these semiautomated techniques is that they use about three times as much labor as the more sophisticated technologies for a given output.

An additional manual operation is included in what can be called a nonautomatic procedure. Instead of using conveyor belts between the several hand-fed machines, the materials can be carried in boxes from one work station to another. As soldering is the most difficult part of a totally manual operation, airtight cans would require the efforts of skilled workers. On the other hand, a wide range of nonairtight cans can be produced manually much more easily. A final and important point is that the use of non-automatic machinery, especially when it is simple and second-hand, may minimize investment costs to the extent that low levels of output will not suffer from diseconomies of scale.[81]

The dangers of plant mechanization are illustrated in the case of a can factory in Tanzania in which the main production lines were almost entirely automated and other labor-saving measures were taken. These included placing machines closer together to save on manual transportation of materials between operations, the use of fork-lift trucks, and the greater use of pallets for storage to eliminate much of the handling of individual cans. The result was that, despite four years of government, union, and worker resistance, the labor force was reduced by some 20 percent.[82]

The *food-canning industry,* while potentially a large employer of un-skilled workers in material preparation and can filling, does require a certain minimum amount of mechanical equipment. Generally, commercial canneries have at the least a small syruper, an exhauster, and a double seamer for closing cans, and in addition the entire unit is usually coupled together so as to avoid the handling of hot cans until they have been sealed. The difficulties involved in the manual handling of hot, open, liquid-filled cans make this unit almost a necessity. The need for precision in closing the cans also indicates the practicality of mechanizing this process as well.[83]

On the other hand, labeling, casing, and subsequent handling can be performed manually on any scale. Although at times there may be a slight cost advantage to automating these processes, the use of human labor insures a far superior inspection of can and labeling imperfections. Furthermore, in those plants where cans of varying sizes are used, the "down time" involved in adjusting machinery makes manual handling preferable.

The choice of technology in the *soft drink bottling industry* should be determined by the size of the market involved. Small, hand-fed, hand-operated filling and crowning machines operating at low output rates were once widely used in the United States, but they are no longer economically feasible. Lower wage rates in Latin America may make the use of these techniques practical in some instances. On the whole, however, the most labor-intensive technologies available should be ruled out primarily for reasons of quality control. High sanitary standards are difficult to maintain when most plant operations are done by hand. Hand washing and hand filling of bottles are the greatest potential labor-absorbers, but the former activity in particular is a major cause of sanitation problems. It is suggested that modern equipment be used from the beginning because of the importance of making a high quality product and the rapid growth of markets, which is a salient characteristic of this industry.[84] Perhaps an acceptable compromise would be the use of an intermediate technology, which includes a bottling machine but leaves the loading and unloading of crates to manual labor. This would more than double the number of workers employed in the most modern plants.[85]

While *cement* production is basically a capital-intensive process, greater mechanization and automation (better plant organization, installation of conveyor systems, introduction of continuous-flow methods) have led to even further elimination of unskilled labor in modern plants. An abundant supply of such labor and high capital costs should rule against the introduction of expensive conveyor systems, although a short supply of more skilled workers can be supplemented with automatic control devices. Compared to other industries, cement production requires less professional and technical personnel in relation to the amount of employment it can potentially offer semiskilled and unskilled workers.[86]

Recent technological modifications have permitted a significant scaling-down of capacity without a loss of efficiency. The Chinese rely upon small-sized plants using simple vertical kilns for the sintering process—as opposed to large plants utilizing conventional rotary kilns—for almost half their national output.[87] A policy of small-scale cement production would increase employment opportunities, as it has been found that the number of laborers per ton of output begins to decrease markedly after reaching a rather low level of output.[88] Smaller-scale production for small markets could also involve more workers in the distribution system. In addition, labor-intensivity can be raised somewhat in plants with multiple- rather than single-unit production. Yet while smaller machines require more operator time per unit of output, the demand for labor in this industry remains relatively small in proportion to the volume of output.[89]

An example from the *wood-making industry* is offered by Ranis. He explains the labor-intensive methods used in Korea in plywood production:

In the manufacture of plywood, what at first appears as production processes very similar to those carried on in the United States, that is, fixed proportions, in fact turn out to be quite feasible—interestingly enough mainly because of the greater machine speed combined with much more labor-intensive repair methods used. In the United States, defective pieces of lumber are cut out automatically by machine and discarded. In Japan, defective pieces of lumber are cut out by hand and the section is discarded. In Korea, defective sections are cut out by hand, the scraps saved, and the defect plugged manually. Here, once again, a lower quality raw material can be upgraded through the application of cheap labor. Consequently, overall, there are twice as many workers per unit of capital equipment in Korea .... At the same time, in the production of Korean plywood, between 10 and 15 percent more workers are engaged in inspection, repair, and maintenance of both materials in process and the machinery in place.[90]

Ranis also examines the Asian *electronics industry*, which has great relevance for Latin America where the industry has experienced rapid growth. In Korea, a number of steps have been taken in the direction of greater labor utilization in transistor assembly operations. Machinery is run six days a week and three shifts a day, that is, to its full physicial capacity. Feeding and packaging operations are usually not done automatically, but rather by hand on an assembly line. There are additional women employed in testing, inspection, and repair efforts, with defective pieces repaired by hand instead of being discarded. And a considerably larger maintenance and repair staff is required because of the full-capacity use of the machinery.[91]

Electronics assembly operations in Taiwan make intensive use of labor, mainly women, to replace automatic techniques. Ranis found this to be true in interviews with various companies:

According to the general manager of one major electronics firm, the amount of labor used in assembling one television set in the Taiwan plant is 50 percent greater than that in a plant of the parent company in the United States. In fact, most of the electronics firms interviewed were making efforts in one way or another to introduce labor-intensive methods.[92]

This suggests that, despite a growing technological sophistication and consequently higher labor productivity, the capital/labor ratio in this industry need not increase and can even decline as it apparently did in the 1960s.

The *steel industry* is an example of an area in which the use of the most modern technology is almost a necessity, and little labor substitution appears feasible. Although small-scale technologies, that is, small backyard furnaces, are available, modern steel mills produce steel so much more cheaply and of so much higher quality that they are also most appropriate for the Latin American region.[93] Even as part of a full-employment strategy, it would seem foolish, given the relatively small increase in jobs involved and the sacrifices that would be made in product quality and economic growth, to use other than capital-intensive production techniques.

SUMMARY

It is apparent that most industries, both traditional and modern, lend themselves to more labor-intensive production than is commonly assumed. Even in continuous-process industries, where greater labor utilization is limited in the central manufacturing process, ancillary operations—which usually constitute a major part of a total production process—can absorb significantly more workers. Smaller-scale production can also result in greater employment generation in plant operations, as well as in distribution. In many industries, the implementation of such production policies on a large scale would have a great employment impact without sacrificing competitiveness in product cost or quality. Our examination of a wide range of manufacturing industries lends support to this view, while demonstrating that claims of technological fixity are greatly exaggerated.

4 ECONOMIC FACTORS
IN THE CHOICE OF TECHNOLOGY

As was shown in Chapter III, the influence of "technological fixity" upon the choice of production techniques is much overrated; thus, the bent toward labor-saving methods must have other causes. Among the most potent of these are economic—primarily the existence throughout Latin America of a set of distorted prices on the factors of production. Faced with a situation of underpriced capital and overpriced labor, many an entrepreneur has made an investment decision which, though perhaps rational in business terms, is totally inappropriate for a country that has a chronic shortage of jobs for its masses of unemployed. The situation is made more difficult and confused by an unjustified emphasis upon worker productivity.

THE QUESTION OF LABOR PRODUCTIVITY

One of the major explanations offered by public and private sources in Latin America for the limited absorption of the labor force into full-time employment is the need to maximize productivity, especially in the modern industrial sector. The general rationale behind this emphasis on labor productivity centers on the requirements for investment funds for future growth and for lower prices on output so that it can compete, particularly in export markets.

The first argument has been analyzed and refuted in Chapter I. High returns to capital are not necessarily translated into the financing of activities in the national interest. A large portion of the profits leave the country in one form or the other; others are reinvested domestically in speculative activities that can be considered neither socially nor economically productive. On the other hand, there is potential for considerable savings by the poor if they were the recipients of a greater share of the national income and were provided with the appropriate savings institutions.

The second argument ignores the possiblity that the nation's output can be produced more efficiently if its inputs are in line with the country's relative factor endowments. Except in cases where there is yet no technical way to manufacture the product in question in other than a highly mechanized manner, it would be incorrect to assume that it could not compete in international markets if it were to have a high labor content. Indeed, as argued earlier, an abundant supply of potentially cheap labor should be viewed as an asset, which, when utilized to its fullest, optimizes the efficient employment of all resources at such a country's disposal.

The issue is confused by the fact that the term "productivity" has become identified with maximizing output per worker. This is logical in the case of most developed countries, but not in Latin America where unskilled labor is an abundant resource. The importance of labor productivity should be de-emphasized, as the ILO's report on Colombia suggests:

We have carefully considered the implications a decrease in the rate of growth of labour productivity would have for Colombian modern industry from the point of view of its capacity to compete in foreign markets. . . . We concluded that this effect would not necessarily, indeed not probably, impair the Colombian capacity to increase exports of manufactures. . . .[1]

Nonetheless, efforts to raise labor productivity in Colombia's modern industrial sector have persisted to the point where it is now almost twice as high in that sector as in any other. The same is true in most other Latin American countries,[2] where preference is given to the upgrading of the skills of employed workers rather than to the hiring of additional personnel. As a result, while manufacturing output has increased rapidly, the rate of job creation has been much lower; some estimates place the elasticity of output with respect to labor at approximately three in many developing countries.[3]

To the extent that capital is available and relatively inexpensive, growth in labor productivity in certain modern industries does allow for a rise in exports and thus for an absolute growth in the economy. More jobs are thereby created but, because of the capital intensivity involved in the productive process, the economy has not benefited from the growth in employment that might otherwise have been generated. Moreover, the greater the amount of investment made in the modern manufacturing sector, the more rapidly craft industries are eliminated. The loss of labor-intensive industries that are incapable of competing with the modern sector because of managerial deficiencies and limited access to capital at preferential rates aggravates the unemployment problem considerably.

This raises a very basic question: for whose benefit is labor productivity being increased? While this productivity, resulting from capital attained at artificially low rates, can lead to a rapid growth in the economy, it also fosters a stagnation in the growth of employment. The wages paid in the urban modern sector have risen substantially, but those workers represent only a small portion of the labor force and may, in fact, support several unemployed relatives. Meanwhile, the bulk of the labor force remains at low levels of productivity and income.

If the productivity of labor is to become a measure of true economic development for *all* members of society, it should be taken as an average for the entire population.[4] Preference should be given to raising marginally the productivity of all available members of the labor force rather than to increasing that of a relative few. A situation of full employment should be the goal, and the meaning of productivity should be reevaluated in light of the circumstances that exist in a labor-abundant, capital-scarce economy.

THE OVERPRICING OF LABOR

Much of the concern with labor productivity can be attributed to the malalignment of factor prices in Latin America. The availability of capital at rates below those that accurately reflect its scarcity and a price of labor above that which reflects its abundance give the entrepreneur both an incentive and the means to maximize the productivity of his work force. The result is a general tendency to introduce labor-saving technological processes into economies with massive amounts of un- and underemployment.

In those sectors of the economy in Latin America in which minimum levels of wages and benefits are established through labor legislation, the cost of labor to the employer is usually considerably more than the relative magnitudes of supply and demand would indicate. This phenomenon can be explained in several ways. For one, many employers are willing to pay what it takes to obtain a steady, reliable work force. In addition, compensation is provided for the higher living costs in urban areas. Furthermore, the shortage of skilled workers and their subsequently high salaries push up the wages of all those in the modern sector. The main causes, however, have been political in nature.

The interests of governments, business, and labor unions have conveniently coincided to the detriment of the unskilled, nonunionized worker. Many of the populist leaders of the past few decades created a loyal following among the working classes of the large cities by sharing generously with them the fruits of the nation's growth. They realized that urban workers constituted an element in the population which was growing in size and importance and which, when organized into unions, was likely to have a degree of discipline and unity that many other parts of the constituency lacked. It was therefore in the interest of these leaders to cultivate the support of the unions and seek a degree of control over their activities by supplying financial assistance to their organizations.[5]

The unions' bargaining positions are strengthened by both this political leverage and by a common government policy of protecting the domestic market. This policy helps not only companies operating within that market, but their employees as well. With competition limited, enterprises are able to raise their prices and thus absorb high capital costs and accept union wage demands.

The widespread use of collective bargaining in Latin America, however, makes it difficult for firms to take on a larger number of the unemployed at more realistic wage levels. It does not generally appear that organized labor is very concerned about the unemployment problem. Victor Alba suggests that the sense of responsibility toward society present in European workers is largely lacking among Latin Americans. He goes on to explain that:

the continent's tradition of labor struggle is generally an unimpressive one, and the imported traditions, a shaky foundation at the outset, tended quickly to be forgotten. Moreover, unemployment and economic crisis were never as serious in Latin America as in the U.S. and Europe. And in any case there was always the option of returning to the villages, a process that led naturally to alleviating the harshness of such a period. There is, therefore, among the masses no sense of heritage in organized labor, and no notion of the individual worker as a responsible participant in society. Their ignorance of both notions has led both worker and union to an indifference to the general interests of society.[6]

Less than 20 percent of the Latin American work force is enrolled in unions, and they use the tools at their disposal to widen the financial gap between themselves and the masses of less advantaged workers.[7] In Colombia, the income of workers in the modern manufacturing sector is roughly three times that of those employed in the craft-manufacturing and agricultural sectors. This is in large part a result of the doubling of real wages in the modern sector in the late 1950s and early 1960s.[8] During that time, small craft firms were able to compete because minimum wage legislation did not effectively cover them. Eventually, however, improvements in management and the greater accessibility to credit for the modern firms made competition by traditional enterprises exceedingly difficult. Indeed, as Reynolds and Gregory point out in the case of Puerto Rico, the small companies that failed during that period did so primarily because of managerial deficiencies, not because of rising wages.[9]

As the ILO suggests in the case of Colombia, it would be unjust—and also politically infeasible—to try to resolve the unemployment problem by reducing wages in the modern sector. Although real wages have risen considerably since the 1950s, this followed a period over which they hardly rose at all in Colombia and elsewhere on the continent. On the other hand, wage increases should be maintained within limits, not necessarily corresponding to rises in productivity but, rather, to escalations in the cost of living—as has been the policy in Brazil. Unfortunately, this is generally not the case. Wages pushed upward by the noneconomic factors discussed earlier often contribute to the tendency of entrepreneurs to increase the level of mechanization in their plants which in turn allows them to pay a smaller number of workers relatively high wages.

Wages alone, however, are not behind the antilabor bias in the choice of technology. Fringe benefits are far higher relative to base pay in Latin America than is generally the case in the more developed countries. The source of much of this paternalism is cultural in nature, but the benefits are also granted as protection against potential disruptions of operations. At the same time, a good many of them are either demanded by the unions or required by law.

The benefits range from social security, severance pay, and profit-sharing to allowances for health, education, housing, and transportation to payment for time on sick leave, vacations, Sundays and holidays, and for the nonexistent "thirteenth month." Their magnitude varies from as little as one-third of basic wages in some Central American countries, to over one-half in Venezuela, and to as much as or more than two-thirds in Colombia, Brazil, Peru, and Uruguay.

Labor becomes particularly costly to management when contributions to social security funds are based on the amount of wages paid. Since in most Latin American countries the minimum wage is high in relation to the shadow price of labor and the contributions must be made by both management and labor, there is reason for the former to lean toward more labor-saving production techniques. This preference is even more understandable in those countries in which payroll taxes are levied. In economies in which capital is the scarcest productive factor, it would appear far more sensible to tax its use rather than that of labor.

Job security laws and severance pay are obstacles to employment in many countries. In some, an individual cannot be dismissed after he has been employed for thirty days without being paid exorbitant compensation. Frequently, the result is the development of a large pool of unskilled workers who move from one temporary job to another, never receiving adequate training and thus never becoming qualified for more secure positions.[10] In

Colombia, another consequence of the stringency of job security legislation has been the hiring of workers on a contract basis through outsiders, thereby eliminating all their protection under the country's labor code.

Perhaps even more worrisome has been the natural reaction on the part of management in that country to keep the number of employees to a minimum. Colombian law stipulates that, at the end of a sixty-day probationary period, an employee cannot be dismissed without "just cause," which is often difficult to establish before a labor court. To the employer, therefore, the recruitment of a worker represents a considerable risk; he must either keep him on when there is no longer work for him or pay him indemnity—often of a large sum. The ILO relates that the provisions on dismissal were those most often mentioned by businessmen as impeding the expansion of employment in the private modern sector.[11]

Many companies find it cheaper to bring in additional equipment than to recruit and train the required numbers of workers. Such decisions are often made in light of relatively high rates of turnover and absenteeism. In Puerto Rico, these two factors were considered the principal problems in the industrialization program. A survey of sixty-seven plants indicated that the turnover rate was over 50 percent. A study of a particular textile firm showed an annual turnover rate of 45 percent and a rate of absenteeism close to 7 percent, necessitating the carrying of 115 extra workers as learners or spares for the normal work force of 300.[12]

Biases against the use of labor can also originate from perceptions of, among other things, the possibility of strikes, the unpredictability of labor efficiency, apathetic attitudes on the part of individuals vis-à-vis their job responsibilities, the lack of managerial capacity to handle a large work force, and physical conditions on the job that might impair performance. Any one of these factors might make training costs appear unwarranted and the use of machines attractive.

The introduction of labor-intensive technologies may encounter a more formidable obstacle in the form of a shortage of the necessary skilled personnel. People are needed who can read blueprints, set up tools, maintain production levels and quality standards, and maintain and repair the equipment when needed. Often this machinery is second-hand and, in light of the human resources available, may not be preferable to newer, more expensive equipment. It should be pointed out here, however, that labor-intensive technology need not appear in the form of second-hand machinery; in fact, advantages will be presented in Chapter V for its development in other forms.

The difference between sophisticated, capital-intensive processes and operator-paced, labor-intensive activities is that the former usually require minimal operators' skills but high levels of planning coordination and maintenance capabilities, while the latter demand greater operating skills for adjusting tolerances, pacing the feeding of materials, and controlling quality.[13] These latter tasks, however, can be done by either skilled workers with very little supervision or by unskilled workers with a great deal of supervision. Increased supervision can compensate for a worker's lack of expertise in particular processes or for deficiencies in coordinating activities.[14]

The problem is that good supervisory personnel is extremely difficult to find in Latin America. Individuals from the management class rarely care to perform this function, and those from the working ranks generally lack the education and experience for such a role. Furthermore, societal factors are involved, including the continued tendency of workers to view the manager as the person in charge. This particular problem is exacerbated quite often by the reluctance of management to delegate any authority to the supervisor.

The shortage of supervisory personnel is often cited by managers as a principal reason for a high degree of plant mechanization. A viable alternative in many industries, however, is the utilization of a machine-paced operation, maintaining a relatively low level of mechanization and permitting the use of unskilled in place of skilled labor. While this should raise the ratio between capital and labor costs, the number of workers required should not necessarily diminish and, in some instances, may actually increase. On the other hand, there are many cases in which the market does not demand high product quality, thereby making the choice between a search for better supervisory personnel and a change in production techniques unnecessary.

THE UNDERPRICING OF CAPITAL

Another factor that encourages the use of labor-saving technologies is the underpricing of capital throughout most of Latin America. Interest rates are usually set at levels that do not accurately reflect the scarcity of capital, particularly in light of the quantities needed to fully absorb all the members of the labor force. Although these rates may at first glance appear high, inflation in many countries makes the real cost of capital quite low. In fact, at times the rate of interest has been less than the rate of inflation.

Recent policy in Brazil exemplifies this phenomenon. The cost of money for industrial and commercial borrowers rose steadily in the 1960s, until it reached an effective rate of as much as 4 percent a month by 1969. Even when deducting the rate of inflation, the real cost of capital was rarely less than 20 percent annually. In June of that year, the government acted to reduce the real cost of borrowing to less than 10 percent. For those sectors considered to be of primary importance—such as exporting—interest rates became effectively negative.[15]

Money has continued to be available on good terms for the requirements of industry. The government's goal has been to provide credit at a real cost of 6 percent per annum in order to induce the use—and hence the manufacture—of domestically manufactured sophisticated machinery and equipment. To that end, it has taken steps to streamline the financial system and to force its member institutions to lower their interest rates and operational costs.[16] Use of a monetary correction mechanism has assured that the commercial rate remains above the rate of inflation.

Despite this concerted and successful attempt on the part of the Brazilian government to meet the demands of modern industry for cheap credit, 6 percent money (in real terms) is still expensive by Latin American standards. In Colombia, nominal interest rates have increased significantly of late but lag well behind the soaring inflation rate, with no monetary mechanism operating to correct the imbalance. Similarly, in Venezuela, the price level has risen sharply, surpassing the prime lending rate. The result has been negative effective interest rates in both countries—a condition experienced elsewhere on the continent and one that gives added incentive for capital-intensive investment in a capital-scarce, labor-abundant area.

As in the case of Brazil, there is a tendency throughout the continent to favor the modern industrial sector with the cheapest credit terms. With limited funds at their disposal, banks naturally prefer to lend to the larger and better-established companies. This minimizes both the risks and the number of loans to be extended, thereby cutting down on administrative costs. As a consequence, small enterprises, which tend to be more labor-intensive, often have difficulty in obtaining the credit they need. Even those that are successful usually receive their capital on terms so disadvantageous that they can no longer remain in competition with their more capital-intensive counterparts in the modern sector.

Policies need to be implemented that would provide firms in the traditional manufacturing sector with their capital requirements. In the absence of such policies, a general rise in lending rates would better enable them to compete with larger, more mechanized operations. Although the latter would still be favored in the rationing of funds, the increased cost of capital would reduce their profit margins. Furthermore, to the extent that high rates would discourage the investment in machinery, employment would be increased in the modern industries and stabilized in the traditional, as the latter would find more funds available for their essential investments. In addition, higher interest rates, by themselves and by working against inflation, could generate higher levels of savings and thereby levels of capital formation adequate in the long run to absorb a far greater proportion of the labor force.

Latin American governments might follow the example of several Asian countries which took such steps and have been rewarded with both higher employment rates and a more rapid overall development of their economies. Japan is the greatest success story, and she has been followed by Korea and Taiwan, which have allowed interest rates to rise to 30 percent or more. Taiwan, spurred by the promise of U.S. aid, implemented liberalization policies in the 1960s. Factor prices were realigned and there resulted a dramatic expansion of labor-intensive manufacturing. Significant labor-using innovations took place in the textiles, electronics, and food-processing industries. An export drive was initiated, and the economy began to develop rapidly. A similar pattern was followed in Korea, where a devaluation in 1964 and a major interest rate reform the next year led to substantial changes in technology.[17]

The implementation of comparable programs in Latin America, however, would not be without its problems. Social security legislation in most countries has made the use of labor a more expensive proposition than is the case in Asia. Latin American countries also compare unfavorably with their Asian counterparts in terms of entrepreneurial capacity, educational levels, and levels of technical competence.[18]

More jobs might also be created in industry through other changes in policy. Accelerated depreciation allowances encourage the purchase of new equipment, whereas the elimination of such allowances would certainly force a reconsideration of one's mode of operation. Likewise, tax holidays and other preferential tax treatment now offered for capital use could be turned around to reward firms for increasing the number of employees on their payrolls. In the case of Brazil's Northeast, for example, this turnabout in emphasis would be far more likely to make reduced unemployment a concomitant of industrial growth than do present provisions and policies.

Changes might also be made in policies that presently encourage the importation of new, capital-intensive machinery. Overvalued exchange rates, the existence of multiple and preferential rates, tariff exemptions, and a host of other measures today make the employment of foreign capital goods far more attractive than would be the case if market forces were allowed to operate freely.

An overvalued exchange rate has two principal effects: it lowers the price of foreign goods, but it also reduces the amount of foreign exchange available with which to make these purchases. In Latin America, where foreign exchange rationing tends to favor capital equipment over other imports, the artificially low cost of foreign machinery thus becomes another inducement to entrepreneurs to automate their plants. In countries that have overvalued exchange rates, high rates of inflation, and a history of devaluations, companies have reason to make excessive purchases of foreign capital goods well before they might otherwise have considered taking such action.

In the mid-1950s, the Colombian government used its exchange rate in the development of its economy when the price of coffee in world markets began to fall. In 1957, the crisis peaked and the value of the peso depreciated dramatically. Over the next few years, the system of multiple exchange rates reflected a policy of support of coffee prices and the fostering of a viable manufacturing sector. Devaluations in 1962 and 1965 and the exchange reform of 1967 reduced to some extent the bias toward capital goods imports, but Colombia's exchange rate is still too high to discourage substantial importation of labor-saving equipment.[19]

Tariff policies of most Latin American governments exacerbate the problem. Most tariffs discriminate against the importation of the more labor-using, second-hand equipment, thereby encouraging the purchase of new, capital-intensive machines. This trend becomes more pronounced as a program of import substitution moves from the labor-intensive fabrication stage to that of assembling consumer durables into more integrated forms.[20]

The Brazilians, for example, offer exemption from import duties to those purchasing machinery and equipment, as long as no similar goods are produced domestically. The outright elimination of these exemptions would be an even stronger inducement to the domestic production of machinery. This realignment of relative factor prices could also be expected to encourage more labor-intensive production of these capital goods.

Policies on foreign exchange and import restrictions have promoted in another, more indirect manner, the use of capital-intensive technologies. By protecting domestic industry against outside competition, governments have reduced the incentive for technological changes and the more efficient use of scarce resources. Local producers who enjoy monopolistic advantages and an inelastic demand for their output can withstand inefficiency in their operations and high production costs by raising their prices.

Under these conditions, a firm often remains uncompetitive in international markets much longer than could be justified by its one-time infant status. With its profitability assured in the small, protected, domestic market, a company is able to employ automated plant and equipment highly inappropriate for the size of the market and the relative costs and availabilities of labor and capital. Economic criteria become less relevant and engineering biases are given greater opportunity to manifest themselves.

The consequences of not adapting or developing appropriate production techniques are at least twofold. First, there is frequently an underutilization of industrial capacity which, in a situation of relative capital scarcity, severely damages the economy as a whole. Second, innovational sluggishness perpetuates the low rates of labor absorption in the industrial sector. The hopes of promoting industrial employment by the development of indigenous research, development, and engineering capacities have been stifled by strategies of import substitution. Even subsidies and other forms of incentives—such as low interest rates on loans for research and development—can have only a marginal effect in a protected seller's market.[21]

Import substitution was a necessity in many Latin American countries during World War II and became a common policy on the continent during the 1950s. The first items generally produced under these programs were consumer goods. These entailed comparatively small-scale operations and the employment of a large amount of unskilled labor.[22] During the 1960s, however, the import-substitution process increasingly included capital-intensive industries, and the demands for unskilled labor consequently diminished.

Toward the end of the decade, some countries began taking steps to reverse their protectionist policies. Rarely, however, were they motivated by employment considerations. The Brazilians have reduced import duties in the hope of generating greater exports through increased domestic industrial efficiency. Similarly, the Venezuelans, fearful of the possible consequences of an overdependence on oil, are moving away from the import-substitution stage because the small size of the domestic market is beginning to impinge upon a high growth rate in manufacturing.

The likelihood is that policies of protectionism will be less prevalent in Latin America during the 1970s, but their disappearance will certainly not come overnight. Time will be needed to allow presently inefficient enterprises to make the managerial and technological adjustments required for their competitiveness in world markets. Furthermore, one cannot expect the immediate relinquishment by political forces of the direct controls that protectionist policies provide. Hence, it may be quite awhile yet before the employment-retarding aspects of import-substitution programs are eliminated.

SUMMARY

A firm establishing manufacturing facilities in Latin America is confronted with an economic environment composed of a set of contradictions. Capital is scarce, but large, modern enterprises have access to cheap credit and foreign exchange and can also benefit from accelerated depreciation allowances and from tariffs that favor the importation of modern machinery. There are millions of un- and underemployed throughout the region. yet wages in the modern industrial sector are relatively high and fringe benefits add substantially to the total wage bill. These distorted factor prices reinforce other biases toward capital-intensive production, which may increase the productivity of a company's work force but also limits the participation and thus productivity of a total national labor force. Vested political and economic interests have strengthened the position of labor unions at the expense of the jobless and have favored large, modern companies at the expense of smaller, more labor-intensive firms. There may be some real managerial problems associated with labor-intensive production, but they can neither explain nor justify the policies and economic biases that have supported highly mechanized investment.

5 PROCUREMENT OF LABOR-INTENSIVE TECHNOLOGIES

It is clear that the current distortion of relative factor prices in Latin America has contributed to local investment decisions favoring highly mechanized production. What is not clear, however, is whether a realignment of these prices, by itself, would in most cases substantially alter investment patterns. The biases of domestic and foreign investors toward "modern," capital-intensive production are, like those of the engineers who design their plants, generally too strong to be easily changed. The means to overcome them must include a greater flow of information about the availability of more labor-intensive methods, as well as a reorientation of professional training to focus attention upon adaptive technological activity and the development of appropriate production techniques.

OBSTACLES TO LATIN AMERICAN TECHNOLOGICAL DEVELOPMENT

During the early period of Latin American industrialization—indeed, until quite recently—"engineering one's way around problems" was the standard manner of dealing with those conditions peculiar to developing countries. Throughout the 1950s, efforts were made to achieve rapid industrialization through the use of highly automated production methods, similar to those utilized by the already developed nations. While a number of labor-related difficulties were consequently reduced, so necessarily was the number of laborers employed.

Low priority was given to the development of technologies that could yield both high levels of employment and respectable rates of growth. In 1959, Benjamin Higgins discussed the limited range of techniques available to entrepreneurs in developing countries (LDCs). He wrote:

No advanced technology has yet been discovered which is suited to the factor-proportions of underdeveloped countries. Perhaps such a technology does not exist; but it is important to find out. Meanwhile, the lack of technological advance adapted to their factor proportions is a serious obstacle to development of underdeveloped areas. . . .[1]

Furthermore, even in those cases in which a choice of method was possible, many countries did not adopt the most labor-intensive techniques available.[2]

When the Alliance for Progress was founded in 1961, its charter—the Charter of Punta del Este—made virtually no mention of science and technology. Even as late as 1965, Victor Urquidi, former ECLA regional director, could write that:

today, after some thirty years of industrialization, it is doubtful whether [Latin America] devotes more than one-twentieth of 1 percent of its GNP to industrial research. This means that the lessons of modern Western industrialization and of the Soviet rise to power have been largely lost upon the Latin Americans.[3]

Toward the end of the decade, special attention was finally paid to scientific and technological development—most notably at the OAS 1967 Punta del Este and 1969 Viña del Mar meetings. If, however, the proportion of the current OAS budget allocated to science and technology is any indication, the emphasis upon technological change in Latin America is still not great. Latin America still lacks a strong base for its technological development needs.

If Latin Americans are not to rely on technologies developed in and for the developed countries and thus often inappropriate to Latin American circumstances, large-scale investments must be made in indigenous engineering capabilities. While this may slow economic growth in the short run, such investments are essential to longer-term growth and development. A nation that does not possess these creative and adaptive capacities cannot successfully utilize science in solving its social and economic problems.[4]

A major problem is the shortage of engineers involved in industrial research and development (R&D). Colombia produces a large number of engineering graduates annually, but many emigrate to the United States and Venezuela—where salaries are higher—and relatively few of those who remain are employed in R&D.[5] Many, in fact, particularly those educated in the United States, turn to careers in management or politics within a very short time. Similar situations exist in many other Latin American countries. It is not just the pay but also the preference for a more interesting working environment that draws scientists and engineers to the advanced countries. They are attracted by superior facilities, the opportunity for greater intellectual interchange, and more challenging problems.

Within Latin American scientific communities, there persists a preference for basic research. Rather than concentrating on solving practical industrial problems, many scientists devote much of their time and energies working on the more prestigious and glamorous project, which may not necessarily be in the nation's best interests (e.g., development of synthetic fibers). At the same time, most engineers either have a strong distaste for anything but sophisticated technology or, as a result of their education, are blinded to any alternatives. As Hagen writes:

. . . improved Western technical education may be counterproductive, in that it causes the individual to become wedded to modern Western practices and lessens his ingenuity. We do not know much about the degree to which such attitudes are increased by one or another type of education, or on the other hand are latent in the individual because of social attitudes inculcated earlier in life.[6]

It is necessary to learn how to copy, adapt, and improve existing technology before new technology can be successfully created. The United States and the other now economically advanced countries went through this process, and Latin American countries can shortcut it only to their own detriment.[7]

In Latin America there do exist social forces that influence the choice of the glamorous over the mundane, the "modern" and "sophisticated" over the more simplistic, and the highly mechanized over the more practical. Intermediate technology is often thought to represent second-class development, although often it is more appropriate to local conditions than are more "advanced" techniques. These beliefs are frequently reinforced by the training that engineers and economists receive, particularly in the United States. There is a need for the restructuring of schools, both in Latin America and abroad, so that they educate their Latin students to the particular needs and circumstances of their countries, rather than to those that exist in the already developed countries.

The textbooks used today in industrial engineering usually lead staff engineers to favor high levels of mechanization and large volumes of output. Their education and training have often put them in touch with foreign consulting firms and manufacturers, which, because of their lack of experience with factor proportions in Latin America, usually only reinforce the traditional biases. Engineering consultants "usually consider familiar patterns to be satisfactory if they are feasible at all. Technologically, [they] tend to be 'satisficers' with the familiar, not optimizers from among possible alternatives." Once the project commences, they follow the practices employed in industrialized countries, giving little thought to invention or redesign of methods.[8] Even a local engineering firm usually brings this per-spective to the projects it undertakes. It or its foreign counterpart must generally be employed by a local entrepreneur, who has to select a produc-tion technique. The choices presented to the entreprenuer are usually limit-ed and prejudicial against the use of capital-saving methods.

Pickett asserts that it is the entrepreneur or economist who is to blame. He reasons that, given the nature of his training, the engineer's in-terest will be in technical efficiency and he will instinctively automate any plant presented to him. The investment decision, however, "is an engineer-ing one subject to a broad economic constraint" and economists have failed to decisively influence it. According to Pickett, they have generally assum-ed that they make the final decision and have the engineer properly under control, but their conceit blinds them to the fact that they are being pre-sented blueprints for a limited number of (capital-intensive) alternatives. Their view is thus a distorted reflection of what usually happens when proj-ects are appraised in developing countries.[9]

What the conceit of the economist has obscured is the fact that the techni-cal ideal has so rapidly become the actual in developing countries that al-ternative possiblities have been passed by, if not out of ignorance then out of sloth and in the face of well-considered economic grounds for attending to them. . . . If the choice [of technique] seems inappropriate, it does not naturally occur to the economist to suspect the engineer. It does occur in-stinctively to him to suspect someone (governments and trade unions are the favoured culprits) of tampering with factor prices.[10]

Thus the choices made by businessmen may be as short-sighted as the range of technologies made available to them. They, too, are frequently possessed of ignorance and biases, often preferring the old and reliable to the experimental. Some choose to mechanize so as to eliminate labor dif-ficulties. Others do so out of more sympathetic concern. Strassmann[11] de-picts well this state of affairs in many parts of Latin America, one marked more by intentional lack of contact and understanding than by any sadism:

Labor intensity can replace cracked gears with broken toes, and short cir-cuits with blindness. . . One cannot easily teach the rich that over-mechani-zation does social damage. . . . The rich in poor countries do not enjoy the poverty of the poor. They try to insulate themselves from it both psycho-logically and physically. They do it with gleaming automatic machines in their factories and with dense walled gardens in their residential districts beyond strolling distance from slums.

If a firm is operating in a protected market that gives it a monopolis-tic advantage, the entrepreneur's bias toward capital-intensivity is allowed to thrive. These biases are further reinforced by the preferences of consumers. Consumption patterns that are increasingly inclusive of demands for Western-styled goods produced by imported techniques blind the entrepreneurs, as well as the government and populace in general, to the grave unemployment problem that these technologies are perpetuating.

THREE ROUTES TO LABOR-INTENSIVE TECHNOLOGIES

The bent of Latin American engineers, entrepreneurs, and government officials toward the use of sophisticated, highly mechanized industrial processes is, as emphasized throughout this book, counterproductive to the region's socioeconomic development. The necessity of generating employment opportunities through the use of labor-intensive techniques leaves those in a decision-making position with three basic alternatives. First, those methods used during a comparable period in the industrial development of the now advanced countries can be transferred directly for use in Latin America; these usually take the form of second-hand machinery and equipment. Second, "sophisticated" technologies developed overseas can be adapted to fit the conditions of their new environment. Third, new technologies can be designed to best suit those conditions.

In the early stages of their development, the Japanese utilized second-hand machinery from the industrialized Western world in order to accommodate their factor proportions. Today, the Chinese do the same, employing technology used by the Russians during the 1950s. The equipment is certainly available and precedents have been set for its use, but disadvantages do exist.

Many developing countries view this process as an attempt by the developed countries to unload their obsolete techniques on them. This is understandable in light of their past experiences with the advanced countries and the perception of Latin American leaders of what constitutes first-class development. There is also the costly necessity of dismantling and shipping, which makes this equipment less attractive to local entrepreneurs. Furthermore, used machinery is more likely to contain flaws and break down. Its repair can become an expensive proposition and real problems are created in those cases in which the necessary spare parts are no longer produced.

On the other hand, second-hand capital goods are often as efficient as new equipment and obtainable at greatly reduced prices, making purchase of them worthwhile even if maintenance costs are high. There is thus involved a saving of scarce capital and the creation of more jobs. An additional benefit from the use of such machinery is that the need for greater maintenance and servicing can actually generate additional employment.

Often, however, second-hand machinery increases not just the level of employment at a given plant but also total capital costs. This is a result of the development in subsequent years of new materials, which enable new technologies to save on both labor and capital and thereby make old technologies absolutely obsolete. In other words, methods used years ago may be more labor-intensive in that they possess a lower capital/labor ratio than do today's techniques, but they actually utilize more capital per unit of output than do these capital-intensive methods.

In addition to the direct transfer of labor-intensive equipment, more capital-intensive techniques developed in the advanced countries can be adapted to local conditions before they are transferred or before they are actually utilized. At times this may only involve making minor adjustments to accommodate differences in the scale of production. More often, however, it would entail large-scale changes in the production process to allow it to better take advantage of relative local factor prices.[12]

At an early stage of industrial development, it is more in a country's interest to take advantage of the processes developed abroad than to attempt to invent new techniques on its own. Even among the advanced countries, with the exception of the United States, no nation invents more than 10 percent of the new technology incorporated into its industrial sector annually.[13] It therefore makes good sense to concentrate on the development of one's capacity to modify already existing techniques to suit local conditions rather than on undertaking costly and often fruitless basic research.

The Japanese, in addition to using second-hand Western equipment, concentrated their innovational efforts on adapting foreign technology to their particular socioeconomic circumstances. It would appear that this task would be facilitated today for the developing countries by the far greater choice of techniques available, but Latin Americans, at least, are not as capable of responding to these opportunities as were the Japanese. The latter possessed an industrial organization and levels of managerial skills and ingenuity superior to those in Latin America. Education and manpower skill levels were also higher.

Of greater significance is the disparity between the scientific and technological base existing in Latin America today and in Japan at a comparable stage in its development. Japan had a cadre of scientists and engineers with the experience and innovative ability to adapt technologies and stimulate development.[14] Latin America, on the other hand, possesses only a very limited capacity for technological conversion as a consequence of a shortage of qualified personnel and their employment in less essential endeavors.

The importation of industrial techniques may, in itself, stimulate the development of a solid foundation of scientific and engineering capabilities in Latin America. The experience of adapting this technology can be a stimulus to creative activity. Unfortunately, engineers assigned this task are too often reluctant to innovate because of the risks involved, or they often just do not perceive the opportunities available to them.[15]

A reluctance to devote resources to adaptive activity denies a country not only an opportunity to develop innovational capabilities but also invaluable experience in selecting and modifying technology from abroad. In order for a country to effectively utilize foreign expertise, it must develop an ability "to ask questions and to theorize, to experiment, invent, and apply."[16] Thus, while purely innovative activity may not be warranted by its direct yields, it may be justified by the scientific and technological foundation that it builds.

One of the real problems in adapting technology is that so much scientific material has been printed that it is often quicker to undertake a new research project than to check through all the existing literature, particularly if a country does not possess sufficient numbers of trained personnel who know where to look for the relevant information. It is not surprising, therefore, that this second approach is rarely the route chosen.[17] This is unfortunate because the basic research that is done instead is usually devoted, as discussed earlier, to projects more glamorous than the creation of "second-class" production techniques. Furthermore, the distinct possibility exists that work in the creation of new technologies might only become a costly duplication of work already done elsewhere and that even an original design may carry a price tag that far exceeds the benefits to be gained from lower operating costs.[18]

LOCATING R, D & E FACILITIES

The process of technological transfer and adaptation will play a central role for many years to come in the industrial development of Latin America. Imported second-hand equipment has its place but, for reasons discussed above, its use also has its limitations. The creation of new technologies that utilize more labor than do those techniques already available also has its merits, and the innovative experience that it provides is an extremely valuable by-product. Their costly and unpredictable nature, however, usually makes preferable the adaptation of other techniques.

Whether new methods are to be developed or old ones modified, is it better to have this work done in the developed countries or in individual, or groups of, Latin American nations? Because of the concentration of the "centers of engineering excellence" in the former countries, some projects may have to be undertaken there, but the record to date does not hold out much promise that these centers will be effective in dealing with the unique requirements of the Latin American industrial sector. Presently, some 98 percent of world expenditures on technological development takes place within the developed countries, but only one percent of it is allocated to research into the specific problems of developing countries.[19]

Research institutes in the developed countries often suffer from an insufficiency of knowledge of the economic conditions in particular Latin American countries. Even if enough information is available, the institute has rarely had the experience required to deal with these conditions effectively. Furthermore, it is generally handicapped by the logistical difficulties involved in trying to work closely with a client firm thousands of miles away.

Strassmann recommends at least a partial solution to this last problem. He suggests that if it were granted the right guarantee and incentive,

a research institute could adopt a firm, acquire access to its records over a period of time, exchange personnel, communicate apparent technical and scientific possibilities to it, and develop production methods that the firm will be committed to demonstrate to outsiders under a subsidized technical assistance contract.[20]

Among those who are best suited to serve as technical advisors to Latin American companies are the Japanese, who have dealt extensively during their industrial development with the production techniques needed in developing countries today. There is, however, the strong possibility that local firms will become overdependent upon such foreign advisors. The longer this dependence lasts, the more the development of indigenous engineering capacities, and thereby the long-term industrial development of the country, will be retarded. If employment is to be created in the Latin American industrial sector to any significant degree, the countries of the region must utilize and develop these capabilities.

Unfortunately, there are very few research institutes in Latin America that devote their energies to the development of technologies appropriate to local conditions. The Universidad Nacional Autónoma de Mexico is a notable exception. Over the past several years, it has worked in conjunction with Mexican industry to develop and apply methods for adapting to Latin American conditions processes developed for use in the advanced countries. It has also sought to train future decision-makers and innovative designers to be responsive to these conditions, particularly in terms of maximizing the substitution of labor for capital.[21] There is an urgent need to strengthen higher education and develop programs that will make possible the creation or reorientation of more such institutes. In addition, far more substantial funding has to be made available than is presently the case. Because R&D usually accounts for only 5 to 10 percent of the total cost of innovation, it is well worth the additional, although large, expense.[22]

The entire research and development structure of Latin American countries has to be strongly oriented toward solving production problems. To this end, and in light of the poor record of the area's research institutes,[23] it has been suggested that rewards or other incentives be given for innovation in appropriate technology. The inferior patent systems that exist in most of the countries make this recommendation particularly sound.

There are distinct advantages in conducting research within Latin America. In contrast to work done by institutes in developed countries, scientists accustomed to the Latin American environment can test their findings under local conditions. They can also establish direct links with their client firms, dealing with the companies' most urgent problems and receiving immediate feedback. In addition, local institutes can influence industrialists and encourage them to undertake their own R&D and adapt their technologies to local factor proportions. The indigenous research institute might also advise its government on economic matters. It could assist it in planning realistic macro- and micro-industrial measures and could occupy a key position between it and industry, keeping both abreast of the others' activities.[24]

It might be advantageous to set up such institutes on a regional basis, given the high costs involved and the similarities that exist among the conditions in many of the countries. The Andean Pact, for example, calls for such action, and Decision No. 24 of the Andean Group stipulates that internal savings be channeled to this effort.[25] To date, however, little progress has been made on the continent, in large part because of the disagreements that have arisen over where the institutes should be located. Research institutes might better be established under the auspices of other mechanisms of regional cooperation, such as the Regional Development Program of the OAS.

This type of cooperative undertaking would be an effective way of dealing with many of Latin America's scientific and technological shortcomings. But given the unlikelihood of creating such bodies in the near future, in most cases it is still preferable to concentrate industrial R, D, & E (research, development, and engineering) efforts in the region's individual countries rather than relying on the institutes of the highly industrailized nations. As stated earlier, not only are native institutes better placed to develop technologies because of their superior knowledge of local conditions and their proximity to client firms, but they also contribute directly to the region's development by cultivating indigenous R, D & E capabilities.

SELECTION OF APPROPRIATE INSTITUTIONS

In a given Latin American country, there are several bodies within or contiguous to which an industrial research institute can be organized. These include universities, government agencies, independent centers, industrial associations, domestic firms, and subsidiaries of foreign companies. Universities, however, are not usually a viable alternative, despite the disproportionately large amount of technical talent concentrated in them. While the educational process might gain somewhat from the stimulus that fundamental research would provide within university environs, the benefits to the industrial sector would be few.

In the early stages of industrial development, research activities should be focused on finding answers to practical problems. Industry requires quick solutions to any difficulties that might arise and these are generally the types of problems that university scientists find uninteresting. The latter are usually interested in academic careers and the opportunity to research without time constraints; they are generally not oriented toward applied research and its inherent demands for continual results. Moreover, university research installations have frequently been designed for teaching purposes and may not be suited to meet the needs of the industrial community.[26]

There is also the problem of relationships with the government. Traditionally, university researchers have not interacted effectively with government agencies. Furthermore in many Latin American countries there exist antipathies between university and government because of student protests. The difficulties that arise as a consequence range from strikes, which close down the school and research activities, to government reprisals in the form of reduced funding.

Nor are government institutes the best location for industrial research. During the initial stage of industrial development, the absence of other institutions forces the government to play a central role, and it is likely that it will always remain involved—at least to the extent of financing research by other bodies. As industrial development progresses, however, lack of direct contact between industry and government agencies can severely limit the latter's effectiveness. There is also the possibility of governmental interference with its institute's work for political purposes.[27]

Another disadvantage to using a government research institute is the uncertainty that the research results and other company secrets will be kept confidential. The commonly held view of governments that patents interfere with the use of knowledge does in itself make such institutes rather unsuited for satisfying a company's needs. Furthermore, government institutes seldom actively seek private contracts. The result is usually, as is documented by Strassmann in the cases of Mexico and Puerto Rico, a tendency of industrial firms not to utilize government research services when other alternatives are available to them.[28]

The very inefficiencies or the absence of a patent system in many places in Latin America, however, often makes necessary an active governmental role in developing appropriate technologies. Its direct or indirect involvement is also frequently necessitated by economies of scale in R&D. Where many small firms cannot hire full-time people, the government can create a pool of technical expertise to be available at its own institutes or at those private institutions which it assists. The advantage of providing this service directly through a government agency is that the work can be adjusted to meet the requirements of the country's development program. In order to induce reluctant companies to utilize these technical services, however, it might be necessary to make their use a prerequisite for obtaining credit from government institutions.[29]

There is also room for agencies independent of government and industry. Often these technical institutes overemphasize research and specialize in their own chosen field. Such foundations are frequently nonprofit and supported by the government, as it is not common to find firms in Latin America that are willing and able to commit resources to such efforts. This type of institute is useful in situations where it can fill a gap left by other institutions.[30]

Baranson suggests that process and equipment design capabilities be largely concentrated in the hands of local consulting engineering groups.[31] The advantages here are the ability of the group to work closely with an individual company, deal with its practical problems, and maintain the relationship on a confidential basis.

It is unlikely, however, that local firms will take the initiative and either request technological changes from its consultants or undertake such research on their own. Where domestic enterprises are protected against foreign competition, there is little incentive for them to invest in costly R&D efforts. It is far more probable that they will simply purchase equipment from abroad, and often this equipment will not be suited for local conditions.

If the R&D potential of indigenous firms could be mobilized, however, it would have a number of distinct advantages over R&D undertaken at other centers. R&D would be oriented toward practical problems and the needs of industry, including the adaptation of foreign technology. The results of the research could also be rapidly put to commercial use. And such efforts would give an enterprise an advantage over its competitors.[32]

When industrialization is in its early stages, few firms are capable of carrying on their own R&D. As the industrial growth proceeds, however, and companies increase their resources and experience, they can be induced to take over much of this responsibility from the government and other institutions. It is probably better to offer these incentives to associations of industries—particularly if they are small or medium-sized—than to individual companies, in order to effect a wider distribution of technical innovation and maximize the benefits for the entire society.[33]

R, D & E IN MNC SUBSIDIARIES

The place best suited for R, D & E activities, however, may well be the subsidiaries of foreign corporations. They possess both the scale of operations and the technical expertise to justify the cost of independent research capabilities. Few other institutions, with the possible exception of some governments or associations of domestic companies, possess comparable resources. Furthermore, multinational corporations (MNCs) frequently have backward and forward linkages to supplying firms and consumers, thereby multiplying their innovative impact on the economy.[34]

Generally, Latin American governments have viewed the MNC as a major source of highly sophisticated technologies. The role of the MNC, however, should be more than merely that of transfering existing techniques. Rather, it should (or should be induced or required to) consist of both the adaptation of these methods to local conditions and the design of new production systems. This involves the creation of engineering research and product design capabilities at the plant level.[35]

The MNC is also in a position to coordinate the research efforts of the various local institutions, as it possesses an experience in this field that is usually lacking in Latin America. The National Academy of Sciences has recommended[36] that foreign corporations increase their interaction with local governments, universities, research institutes, and other enterprises. The services of university laboratories and other technical agencies should be used whenever possible and their capabilities improved so as to raise the quality of their contribution. One way this could be done is for the MNC to train more technical personnel than it needs itself.

The MNC might also train an excess of managerial talent so that domestic firms can overcome many of their organizational deficiencies. It could also enter into joint R&D ventures with these companies and extend both technical and managerial aid to its suppliers. On its own part, it should reappraise its overseas management and staff, as these people might have been hired at a time when locally based R, D & E was not emphasized. Any new personnel should have a knowledge of local economic conditions and the type of technology that the country's socioeconomic development requires.

Although there exists no comprehensive data, the available information suggests that MNCs rarely adapt their production processes when they transfer them to Latin America. Of the R&D they have done overseas, practically all has been performed so as to scale down production techniques for smaller markets, adapt them to local materials, or adjust them to conform to consumer tastes (especially in the case of food processing).[37] Yet changes of this kind have been carried out infrequently.

Mason, in his study of foreign enterprises operating in Mexico and the Philippines, found that the research efforts of the vast majority of them culminated in only minor adaptations in existing technology.[38] Of greater concern, in light of Latin America's employment problems, is the extremely small amount of R&D that has been undertaken for the purpose of adapting to local factor proportions. Furthermore, a United Nations panel discussion revealed that foreign corporations in Latin America quite frequently do not even carry out a comprehensive feasibility study.[39]

There are few encouraging signs. The Dutch electronics manufacturer, Philips, is, according to Louis Turner,[40] the only major company to seriously apply itself to the development of industrial technologies appropriate to the developing world. Yet the principal adaptations have been related to scaling down production, as import substitution policies have meant foreign production runs which are altogether uneconomic by European standards. A pilot plant was set up in isolation, fifty miles from company headquarters, in order to objectively evaluate the firm's technology. The plant has been kept small and the work force unskilled in order to simulate conditions in developing countries. Although Philips has been successful in the simplification of the assembly process, production has not become significantly more labor-intensive. And again it must be stressed that Philips, in just making a serious effort in the area of technological adaptation, is a relative rarity among MNCs. In general, foreign companies perceive too many obstacles in the way of their accommodating Latin American development needs for them to be counted on to undertake the necessary R, D & E work on their own.

As discussed earlier, the imposition of import restrictions often leads to managerial laxity in those firms being protected. For foreign firms—many of which established subsidiaries in Latin America to escape these very restrictions—protectionism likewise reduces their incentive to maximize efficiency. R&D, particularly if it is costly, becomes far less compelling if a firm does not have to seek a competitive advantage.

Moreover, the small size of most Latin American markets for the products of MNCs does not justify, in the eyes of management, establishment of R&D capabilities in each country. Because of the necessarily large size, and thus cost, of each research unit, it is generally in the interest of a multinational corporation to concentrate its efforts in one location. Decentralization and fragmentation of R&D usually create too many diseconomies to be considered a financially wise policy by MNC managers.

Only occasionally does an MNC find some competitive advantage in locating a segment of its R&D in a developing country. These functions are usually a costly part of its total operations and are justifiable to management only if there is a strong probability that they will lead to greater profits. Added revenues must exceed conversion costs, with a premium included for risk and uncertainty.[41] As research costs soar at home and standards of university education rise abroad, however, research work could well begin to move to less expensive areas close to the production site.[42]

Nevertheless, for the time being, foreign firms are also discouraged from establishing local research centers by the shortage of trained personnel in Latin America. Unless they initiate training programs, MNCs often have to rely upon scientists and engineers from their home country. The procurement of top personnel for this purpose may be difficult, however, as such professionals often prefer to develop "sophisticated" technologies and to perform their work close to the centers of scientific and engineering excellence, which are usually located within the highly industrialized nations.

Foreign corporations also hesitate to make alterations in their production processes because of their desire to maintain high industrial standards. They see this as a necessity if their goods are to compete in world markets. Furthermore, most large international companies are unwilling to downgrade their trademark because of the effect that this might have on their reputation in these external markets. Baranson suggests that "some fresh thinking on special product lines and trademarks designed especially for low-income economies in transitional stages of development may be in order."[43] In his opinion, Latin American decision-makers interested in taking action in this area should seriously consider negotiating with smaller, more flexible foreign firms.

For the most part, however, MNCs do not even consider such adaptive activities because they view the technologies already utilized in the industrialized countries as suitable for use in Latin America. This mentality puts severe restraints on the contributions that these firms can make to the creation of labor-intensive technologies and, in fact, may seriously impede general progress in this direction. On the other hand, the host country may consider any attempts by the MNC to develop these technologies as counterproductive to its perceived needs for a sophisticated, modern industrial sector and for industrial output that can earn foreign exchange. Similarly, the transfer of second-hand machinery from a nonindustrialized country may be perceived by Latin Americans as an attempt to foist second-rate goods upon them, regardless of how well suited such goods might be to local circumstances.

Other serious problems stem from the shortcomings of most of the area's patent systems. Many Latin American governments interpret the present international system as a scheme to favor countries that already possess the vast bulk of the world's technology. A major reason for poor patent protection in the region is the view held by many officials that scientific advances should become public knowledge and not the exclusive property of foreign patentees. There is a great deal to be said for this viewpoint, but in reality it probably retards the region's technological development. The inability or unwillingness on the part of governments to protect the fruits of expensive research lead the MNC to question the value of undertaking such efforts. If foreign firms choose to reduce the resources they commit to research into labor-intensive methods, the development of Latin America will suffer a serious setback.

Brazil is one of the few countries that is trying to improve its patent system. In 1969 a new patent code was introduced requiring that patent and trademark licenses be registered with the government. Even in Brazil, however, patent protection is still weak. The agency in charge of registration is understaffed, particularly in competent technical personnel. Submitting to legal arbitration the question of ownership of a specific technological process or design rarely yields satisfying results. It may take years to receive a judgment and the penalties meted out are not sufficiently harsh to inhibit future violations.[44] The situation elsewhere is generally much worse. It is clear that if Latin American governments wish to exploit the vast resources, experience, and capabilities of multinational corporations for the purpose of developing technologies that can help solve the unemployment and other problems of the region, patent regulations must be implemented that will not deter these corporations from their research efforts.

For the same reasons, Latin American governments should strive to create the political and economic climate that will foster local R, D & E work by MNCs. The erratic nature of government policy toward foreign firms and the unpredictability of economic circumstances make a company reluctant to invest large sums in the development of a local research capability. Only when governments adopt policies conducive to the development of labor-intensive technologies will the foreign corporation begin to consider contributing to this endeavor.

For the reasons outlined above, the MNC is rarely willing to commit itself to substantial R, D & E programs in Latin America. Baranson found in his interviews with executives of forty U. S. MNCs (ranging from representatives of the food-processing to those of the automotive industry) that the overwhelming majority do not foresee much expansion of R, D & E efforts on the part of their Latin American affiliates. They do not perceive any such increase in activity to be in their interest and consider the training of technicians and the establishment of quality-control systems as adequate contributions.[45]

It appears that both the carrot and the stick can and must be applied to the foreign firm if there is to be any hope that it will develop and utilize its innovative potential in Latin America. On the one hand, these often risky and long-term investments might be induced by offering substantial tax concessions to interested parties. On the other, requirements might be imposed making it mandatory that all foreign companies spend a given amount or percentage of profits, for instance, on local R, D & E. In the absence of very strong and specific measures, however, it is highly questionable whether MNCs will develop and transfer new technologies unless they hold an equity position in the recipient firm.

The National Academy of Sciences writes of an even stronger motivational factor for the MNC—a threat to its survival in the region. It states that the future of foreign enterprises in LDCs could depend heavily on "their willingness and ability to join with local agencies, investors, and institutions in addressing these problems [including employment] , particularly through the application of their R, D & E resources."[46]

SUMMARY

There is a critical need in Latin America for labor-intensive technologies that will absorb many of the unemployed in the industrial sector. While such techniques do exist, their use has been limited by a general lack of awareness of their availability and appropriateness or, as is more generally the case, by biases against the utilization of second-hand machinery and against the development of "unsophisticated" production methods. The establishment of local R, D & E facilities can help overcome these engineering biases by focusing efforts upon adaptive industrial activity, as well as upon the development of labor-intensive technologies. Located within Latin America, these institutions would be more sensitive to local economic and social conditions and would facilitate contact with industrial clients. The subsidiaries of multinational corporations may be the best place to do such work, in light of the shortcomings of other local institutions. MNCs possess both the scale of operation and the technical expertise to justify the cost of independent research capabilities, and the impact of their work would be felt throughout the economy as a result of their local linkages and a general demonstration effect. There are few signs, however, that these companies are prepared to commit themselves to substantial R, D & E programs without incentives and pressure from Latin American governments.

6 THE M N C AND EMPLOYMENT

There is no shortage of material dealing with multinational corporations in general, nor with their experiences in the world's economically less developed areas. In this chapter a particular aspect of their interaction with the developing world—the link between MNCs and Latin America's vast unemployment problem—will be examined. To this end, we have already taken a look at the extent to which foreign firms particpate in the development of local R, D & E capabilities. What follows here is a broader look at what they are, should be, and are capable of doing in other aspects of employment generation.

ECONOMIC INFLUENCES UPON TECHNOLOGICAL CHOICE

First, however, it is necessary to examine the economic factors that influence MNCs in this area, causing them, at times, to follow a course of action different from that of their local counterparts. In Indonesia, for example, a far greater proportion of foreign firms use sophisticated technologies than is the case with domestic companies, as the former usually pay somewhat higher wages and have access to cheaper capital from abroad.[1] Walter Chudson has found that MNCs in Singapore tend to favor the use of capital over labor for a variety of reasons, including several nonwage labor considerations. Among these are the strength of labor unions, fringe benefit costs, language and factory discipline problems, and the limited availability of particular labor skills. Furthermore, foreign firms in Singapore claim that labor-intensive methods usually result in higher raw material costs and more poorly finished products, and they prefer to use techniques with which they are familiar.[2]

Chudson indicates that foreign subsidiaries are generally guided in their decisions regarding production technology in developing countries by, in large part, the factor prices they confront in their home countries. Local interest rates and capital availability have only a minimal influence upon their technological choice. For example, Strassmann found in his study of technological change in Mexico and Puerto Rico that local capital and labor costs do not influence an MNC in its choice of basic plant design. Whatever effect they might have would usually materialize after the project has been approved, "either in the nature of second thoughts in detail design or of improvisation after startup."[3] Even these belated responses to local prices are unlikely, however, when the MNC is in a protected market and assured large profits.

In addition to this built-in bias toward methods used at home, it is the investment environment—far more than factor costs—that determines the mode of operation chosen by the foreign firm. The degree of political and economic stability becomes a primary consideration when deciding upon the magnitude of the initial capital outlay. No less important are the size of the market (both domestic and export), government incentives, and other official policies. Those companies interviewed for this study indicated that the policies which had the greatest influence upon their selection of production methods and relative use of capital were those concerning exchange rates, import duties and nontariff barriers, and methods of depreciation.

One reason that relative local factor prices do not have a greater influence on the foreign firm's investment decisions is that the MNC is better placed than the locally controlled company to raise funds at low rates in international markets. Of greater significance, in light of the large proportion of the borrowing it usually does locally, is the ability of the foreign enterprise, because of its relatively large size, to obtain capital on more favorable terms than can its Latin American counterpart in the latter's own financial markets. This bias toward excessive capital utilization is strengthened by the incentives offered MNCs to attract their investment—incentives such as depreciation and tax schemes that favor the use of capital rather than labor.

Despite the usually lower cost of funds attainable in the markets of the developed countries, the foreign subsidiary will generally try to maximize its borrowing in the Latin American country. This is logical in light of the inflationary pressures usually present and the danger of having to repay foreign obligations with a devalued currency, but the practice is often limited by inadequacies in the local medium- and long-term capital markets. Difficulties in floating share issues in Latin America, for example, lead most MNCs to obtain their equity capital from abroad. In this case, currency depreciation is not a factor because the subsidiary is not assuming a fixed obligation.

In most cases, local interest rates have little effect upon fixed investment decisions, as most of the necessary funds are borrowed in the country of the parent company. Interviews with U.S. firms operating in Latin America reveal that large amounts of capital are transferred from parent to affiliate for the latter's use in purchasing their capital equipment in the United States. In effecting this transfer, the MNC produces a ratio between repatriated profits and registered foreign capital that is more acceptable to Latin American governments. On the other hand, foreign companies attempt to maximize their local borrowing for their working capital requirements, and at times practically all their needs are satisfied domestically.

Those company executives interviewed stressed that wage levels, like local interest rates, are usually but a minor consideration in their choice of technology for their Latin American plants, although they become of greater importance if and when a conversion of already established operations is being contemplated. These findings are similar to the conclusions drawn by Chudson from a recent U. N. survey.[4] An explanation offered by respondents in both studies was that labor costs are only a small proportion of total costs for many goods manufactured by MNCs. A recent survey of foreign firms in Chile supports this view, showing that an average of only 16.5 percent of all costs were allocated to wages, salaries, and social security.[5]

As Chudson suggests, this may merely reflect the MNCs' bias against the development and employment of more labor-intensive methods. But this might be overstating the case. It appears that labor costs are simply not as critical as other factors to U.S. corporations in their Latin American investment decisions.[6] Chudson reports that companies engaged in continuous assembly-line operations in the automotive, electronics, and similar industries are far more concerned with the high costs of locally produced components and the small size of their markets. Market size seems also to be a more critical determinant than wage levels in the choice of production techniques for other potentially labor-intensive activities, such as some food processing.

The relative unimportance of wage levels to foreign firms is reflected to a degree in their general willingness to pay higher wages than do their domestic competitors. Many companies engage in this policy as a means of attracting the best members of the labor pool and of establishing good labor relations. In most cases, however, the true cost of labor to all firms—foreign and indigenous—are eventually equalized. The higher salaries that MNCs pay are often compensation for the paternalistic benefits commonly extended by other companies. In the long run, superior training programs of U.S. concerns and the consequently higher skills and productivity of their employees justify the latter's higher pay scale.

Furthermore, U.S. firms frequently select workers who are favorably disposed to training and are less prone to absenteeism or to premature resignation. In general, however, the MNC is operating at a disadvantage in making wage payments, because it is not as familiar as is the domestic firm with the customs, behavior, and expectations of the indigenous work force. While the latter can often locate its operations almost anywhere, the foreign enterprise may be forced to locate in the highly urbanized, high-pay areas out of ignorance of how to adapt to labor market conditions in more rural areas. In addition, the MNC is less likely than its domestic counterpart to risk its reputation and position in the host country by violating minimum wage laws.[7]

While wage rates do not usually have a significant influence on the MNC's choice of technology, other labor factors can. Among those most often cited were high fringe benefits required by law, strikes and other labor union problems, casual leave, absenteeism, high turnover rates, low productivity, and difficulties in firing. Most of the companies interviewed indicated the last as the biggest stumbling block to the introduction of more labor-intensive technologies. As was discussed in Chapter IV, dismissal after a stipulated initial period of employment is extremely difficult and costly throughout most of Latin America and particularly so in the Andean Pact countries. In Peru, for instance, it is virtually impossible to fire a worker once he is hired. And while some local firms are adept at getting around these regulations, foreign corporations are constrained by a lack of knowledge and a greater necessity to abide by government dictates.

On the other hand, difficulties with labor unions pose less of a problem for MNCs than they do for their local counterparts. David Blake reports that:

... the large size and international nature of the multinational employer means that management may be able to absorb pressures and even strikes directed toward one particular subsidiary with very little harm to the whole corporation. Other facilities and profit centers located around the world will continue to work largely unaffected by the industrial dispute. Consequently, the corporation is not as susceptible to the various influence tactics in the arsenal of the trade union. In contrast, a solely domestic manufacturer is likely to feel more sharply the various pressures mounted by a union and may well be more responsive to the union demands. Furthermore, the existence of multiple facilities in several different countries may allow the multinational corporation to shift production in a way which ensures the continuous servicing of important markets and production processes. Again, the domestic manufacturer is not able to do this.[8]

Productivity, absenteeism, and turnover rates also rarely present major problems to the MNC. The assumption might be made that the firms that have the most success in these areas are those which are most selective in the workers they hire and those which have the most effective training programs. A survey of executives from thirty-three U.S. manufacturing subsidiaries in Brazil[9] revealed that Brazilian workers are comparable to U.S. workers in their responsiveness to training and in terms of productivity. Burroughs claims that Brazil produces its office machinery and electronic computer components in the São Paulo area partly because of the high productivity of its labor force.[10]

For those instances in which foreign firms encounter difficulties with their work forces, however, there are several possible explanations. Mordechai Kreinin found that U. S. companies operating in Latin America attributed worker ineffectiveness to low levels of education, training, and experience. Of almost equal significance, according to the 150 respondents to his 1964 survey, were a lack of interest in work and efficiency, laziness, apathy, and shortcomings in motivation, drive, dependability, loyalty, and discipline.[11] Hagen argues, however, that many of the inferiorities of skilled workers actually exist only in the assumptions and prejudices of the foreign manager and that questions of attitude are less relevant in the case of unskilled labor because the quality of work demanded is lower.[12]

Whether these negative features of the Latin American labor force are real or imagined, the effect upon the ultimate selection of a production technique by the MNC will be the same. It is not the true circumstances confronting a foreign firm in the host country that influence its decision-making, but rather its perception of them, a perception that is often colored by years of operating experience in developed countries. And where there is a recognition by management of its limited understanding of local labor intangibles, the solution of merely engineering one's way around the problem is often found to be preferable to learning how to cope with it.

CURRENT ROLE OF THE MNC

In light of the potential that foreign firms have for making a marked contribution to the resolution of the employment problem in Latin America, the decision to avoid rather than confront these difficulties is most unfortunate. To understand the extent of this potential impact, both direct and indirect, it is necessary to appreciate the relative magnitude of their investments and sales in the area. In 1966, direct investments by U.S. manufacturing affiliates alone accounted for approximately 7 percent of Latin America's total GDP.[13] Within a decade, these investments had increased by over 60 percent, despite a sharp decline in new investment during the early 1970s. The upward trend continued again in 1973, with the result that by the end of that year U.S. affiliates had holdings in Latin America with an estimated book value of nearly $15 billion; investments in manufacturing constituted close to half of this amount. United States companies owned manufacturing facilities with an estimated worth of over $2.2 billion in Brazil, $1.5 billion in Mexico, $870 million in Argentina, $600 million in Venezuela, and $300 million in Colombia by 1974. Projections for 1975 indicated sharp increases in such investment in Brazil, Mexico, and Venezuela, as well as in Peru.[14]

Raymond Vernon found that, as of 1964, U. S. firms were already responsible for large portions of sales in particular industries. The sales of their subsidiaries represented almost 20 percent of the total in paper products, nearly 30 percent of chemicals, and close to 60 percent of the region's sales of rubber products.[15] In Brazil, the greatest amounts of foreign capital between 1965 and 1968 were invested in the automotive and chemical industries. At the end of 1970, the Banco Central do Brasil reported that the greatest concentrations of foreign investment in manufacturing were in chemicals, transportation equipment, electrical goods, metallurgical products, food products, and pharmaceuticals,[16] which coincide in good part with today's major Brazilian growth industries.

Total employment by U.S. affiliates in Latin America during the decade preceding 1966 grew from 830,000 to 1,230,000, of whom 475,300 were employed in manufacturing. In Brazil and Argentina, U.S. manufacturers employed 130,300 and 96,000 people, respectively; in the latter, 94 percent were Argentine nationals.[17] Chudson reports that, as of 1966, U.S. majority-owned companies in Latin America had approximately two and one-half times more indigenous than American employees. Of the former, almost two-thirds were wage-earners.[18]

Mason, in his study of U.S. firms in Mexico,[19] found that these companies have a larger proportion of their employees at the factory level than do their domestic counterparts. They tend to use more semi- or unskilled (as well as technical and executive) personnel than do indigenous enterprises; the latter tend to employ relatively greater numbers of skilled workers and professionals, such as accountants.

He also found that, while U.S. companies produce more "sophisticated" products, they do so only slightly more capital-intensively than do local firms. The ratio of the wage bill to capital services, however, was used as the basis for this comparison; this can be misleading because, on the average, American firms pay higher wages than do domestic companies. Nevertheless, Mason reports that the former apparently do not use more equipment per worker than do their local counterparts and that their high level of capital-intensivity may be explained by heavier investment in buildings and inventories.

Mason concludes by stating that "a strong case cannot be made for multinational firms being a major source of the factor proportions problem."[20] While it is difficult to demonstrate a direct link between the willingness of the MNC to pay relatively high wages and the artificially high wage level that prevails in most of Latin America's modern industrial sectors, there is little disagreement over the negative effects that these unrealistically high industrial wage rates have on a society. Their existence encourages, at one and the same time, migration to the urban centers and the replacement of labor by machinery in the very sector to which potential employees are attracted.

Wide disparities in wage levels can cause other economic and social disruptions. In the 1960s, the Mexican government was successful in attracting large amounts of American investment to the border area near the United States. The 25,000 border Mexicans employed in these new factories earn an average annual wage of $1000, while a worker in an indigenous plant usually earns about $360. In addition to the inflationary pressures to which this phenomenon contributes, such a disparity in wages, in the opinion of Louis Turner, "cannot benefit Mexican society or competing Mexican entrepreneurs. It is all too easy for the multinationals to pay wages that, though low enough for their purposes, are widely out of line with standard rates in the rest of the economy."[21]

The MNCs often have a strong demonstration effect in the modern sector because they are frequently leaders in their respective industries. Wage policies and the choice of technology of local firms may represent emulations of practices of their foreign counterparts. There is a strong tendency for local companies to develop a technological dependency upon foreigners rather than develop their own indigenous capabilities. Because MNCs, as a rule, have not correlated their production methods to the factor proportions in Latin America, this will mean a perpetuation of capital-intensive operations in most areas of the continent.

The interconnections between local and foreign companies usually have their roots substantially deeper than the mere copying of technologies might suggest. Beneath the surface relationships lies a power structure that links the privileged and powerful forces in each society. As Urquidi writes, "organized business and labour groups, with rare exceptions, are by the nature of their own privileges in the Latin American society unable to dissociate their attitudes to foreign capital from the prospects of their own particular advancement."[22]

This does not necessarily mean that Latin American policy-makers and entrepreneurs find acceptable a special set of ground rules for the MNC. Article 50 of the Andean Group's Decision No. 24, for example, explicitly states that "member countries will not grant to foreign investors any treatment which may be more favorable than that granted to national investors."[23] Statutes of this sort find support in local business communities. This was demonstrated in a survey of the opinions of some 324 local managers from twelve Latin American countries in 1962-63, which revealed a strong aversion to special privileges for foreign-owned businesses. Some admitted that this might not create an atmosphere conducive to foreign investment, but few of the managers interviewed said that they would be willing to compromise on this point.[24]

These perspectives may constitute a serious obstacle to the simultaneous realization of certain export policies, on the one hand, and the attainment of the high employment levels, which many governments claim as a major objective, on the other. If governments continue to rely on the MNC as a principal earner of foreign exchange and view production in the export sector as generally having to be capital-intensive, there appears to be little chance that they could persuade or compel national enterprises to aid in the resolution of the employment problem through greater utilization of labor in their operations.

Although many foreign firms utilize production technologies that are somewhat older than those presently in use in their home countries, these techniques are still highly mechanized and sophisticated. Particularly if they are manufacturing within a protected market, there is no inducement to MNCs to modify technologies and risk downgrading product quality and their international trademarks for the sake of implementing methods that would employ more workers. Thus, there is a built-in bias toward capital-intensive operations, which is sometimes compounded by the need for sophisticated equipment for product testing and quality control.

Despite this tendency to transfer foreign technology largely unaltered to very different conditions in Latin America, it is obvious from the figures quoted earlier in this chapter that MNCs have absorbed a fair quantity of the continent's unemployed. What the figures do not reveal, however, is the immeasurable number of jobs that are eliminated in indigenous enterprises by the economic impact of foreign firms. The comparative advantages that U.S. companies hold lead local firms to emulate the former's emphasis on heavy mechanization rather than attempt to compete with them by utilizing their superior knowledge and understanding of the labor force.

This is particularly true in the case of unskilled labor. American managers over the past two decades have demonstrated their excellence primarily in two areas—advertising and the use of skilled labor. It would appear senseless to attempt to compete in either area, yet Mason's study, as mentioned earlier, shows that indigenous enterprises, at least in the case of Mexico, employ relatively greater amounts of skilled personnel than do their American counterparts. It thus seems logical that Latin American companies should depend far more on the use of unskilled labor than they do at present.

Foreign firms also usually possess a superiority in overall managerial and organizational skills. These advantages, along with their generally better credit-worthiness and their possession of greater amounts of capital, often discourage small, local entrepreneurs before they can "grow up and succeed."[25] Jon Basil Utley reports that when General Motors built its plant in Peru, it preempted the local money supply, causing considerable hardship to smaller Peruvian enterprises.[26] While the importance of credit—vis-à-vis other inputs—to the small firm is debatable, there is little doubt that the availability of credit at rates substantially below its shadow price gives a distinct advantage to MNCs, given their usual reliance upon large amounts of machinery and equipment. Many countries are becoming increasingly aware of the potential of foreign firms to dominate local money markets. Over the past few years, Brazil, Mexico, and the Andean Pact countries have acted to remedy this situation by pressuring MNCs to bring more funds from abroad.[27]

It should be pointed out that MNCs do not always exploit their inherent advantages to compete directly with Latin American companies. Skillful advertising and differences in product quality lead to product differentiation and to sales in two separate and different markets. Furthermore, some foreign firms choose to avoid competition by introducing an entirely different product. This was the rationale of a large U.S. textile company when it decided to manufacture synthetic goods rather than enter a highly competitive market in natural fiber products. Such differentiated products often compete more directly with imported goods than with the output of indigenous enterprises.

The argument is also frequently forwarded that MNCs involved in productive activity have a positive impact on the overall employment situation because of the linkages they have developed with indigenous suppliers utilizing more labor-intensive technologies. It is true that foreign investment can have significant secondary and tertiary effects. As early as 1957, American firms in Latin America were buying a large portion of their inputs locally, and these ties reportedly deepened over the next decade.[28] By 1966 the expenditures by U.S. manufacturing affiliates in Brazil for inputs from Brazilian companies had reached $652 million. In Argentina such sales that year totalled even higher—$724 million.[29]

When local suppliers are used, however, problems frequently arise. The quality of their products, as well as the materials standards of their inputs, are generally below international standards and their supply is undependable. Consequently, the production costs of the contracting firm often soar and the quality of the finished product is inferior. The maintenance of product standardization becomes difficult, creating problems in after-sales servicing. Furthermore, the MNC must devote a good deal of its financial and technical resources to the assistance of its indigenous suppliers.[30]

It appears, however, that given time many of these difficulties disappear. Ranis, pointing to the experiences of several companies, claims that within two or three years local enterprises can supply components more cheaply than can be achieved through importation or manufacture at the main plant.[31] With quality and cost problems mitigated by technical assistance and operating experience, local content requirements can be imposed without the risk of pushing up the price of the end product or of fostering substandard quality.

The experience of the Sears, Roebuck Company in Latin America is an example of a successful effort to develop local enterprises which has benefited both the purchaser and indigenous suppliers. This program was born out of economic necessity when the Mexican government cut off the importation of most consumer goods soon after World War II. Although a retailer and not a manufacturer, Sears also has high quality and delivery standards and thus saw the importance of upgrading the productive capabilities of its new, local suppliers. By guaranteeing a market to these small firms and extending technical assistance and, at times, pre-production financing, the company has been highly successful in this endeavor. After only six years of following this policy in Mexico, it was purchasing locally, from about 1300 sources, 80 percent of what it sold in that market. Likewise, in Peru, it increased its local-buying content over a period of fifteen years from 20 to 90 percent of its total purchases.[32]

Although such cases can be cited, Mason claims that the local content is usually less for U.S. firms than for local companies.[33] Many American subsidiaries in Latin America are assembly plants using imported parts, and in these cases, the linkage effect is minimal. In other instances, it might even be negative. Such would be the case if an entirely new product, such as a plastic sandal, were to preempt through competition the sale of hand-made sandals using local materials.

Another area in which MNCs are capable of making a contribution is in the institution of training programs. Where employees are taught skills that are necessary, but are in short supply in the nation's economy, and where companies are given incentives to train more such individuals than they themselves can absorb, the effect can be highly beneficial to the society as a whole. Undesirable consequences may be felt, however, should the MNC either require and take on more skilled personnel from the host economy than it trains or instruct an excess of potential employees qualified to work in unnecessarily highly mechanized plants.

MNCs are also credited with providing links to export markets in developed countries to earn sorely needed foreign exchange for Latin American economies. The exports of U.S. affiliates account for a substantial proportion of total foreign sales from Latin America—approximately one-third of total exports and over 40 percent of the manufactured goods sold abroad. Nevertheless, these figures fail to reflect the damage done to national balance-of-payments accounts by the common MNC practice of underpricing that portion of its subsidiaries' output destined for other units of the organization. Nor do they reflect the employment opportunities foregone when possibilities for labor-intensive production of high-quality export goods (see Chapter III) are ignored.

Similarly, the contributions that foreign firms have made in the field of technology have not matched their potential for constructive activity in this area. Although they might adjust their production methods to better suit local conditions and aid in the development of local industries through technological transfers, these firms generally choose to maintain exclusive control over their techniques. According to Baranson, except in those cases in which the MNC has equity interest in, or a subcontracting arrangement with, the recipient company, it has little interest in restructuring and sharing its technological knowledge. United States manufacturers, in particular, also have shown little interest in modifying their products to suit the requirements of Latin American countries, citing an absence of incentives for doing so.[34] To the limited extent that MNCs are adapting their technologies, their activity has concentrated on scaling-down production in light manufacturing industries, such as simpler forms of food processing.

Overall, the record does not speak very well for the propriety of the production techniques utilized by U.S. corporations in Latin America, much less for their dissemination in the region's industrial community. When the issue of technological transfer is looked at on a case-by-case, company-by-company basis, however, it is perhaps understandable at times why more has not been done by the MNC in this area for the development of Latin America. But what is disturbing is the philosophical framework within which its decisions are usually made. The president of an international textile company, which has transferred its technology largely unadjusted from the United States, expresses the view commonly held in the business community that highly mechanized production yields optimum efficiency, high rates of economic growth, and thus, in the long run, the greatest number of new job opportunities.

In some business quarters, this view is dying a slow death. One wonders, however, just how much is actually understood and internalized and how much is simply rhetoric. Take, for example, a paper[35] prepared by Charles Dennison, former vice-president of International Minerals and

Chemicals and a leading spokesman for the American business community in Latin America. At one point, Dennison supports a statement from the Organization for Economic Co-operation and Development (OECD) that

the adequacy of the GNP as a measure of success in economic development is being questioned. In the past, undue emphasis has been placed on this measure. . . . Experts are asking that other factors and especially employment and income distribution be considered equally with GNP as measures of progress in development.[36]

Soon afterward, however, he cites Warren Weaver in making the point that MNCs

are becoming an important and effective instrument for transferring and diffusing technology throughout the world. . . the importance of these transfer mechanisms cannot be overrated. They have been a powerful factor in the world-wide diffusion of technology and have brought important benefits to the recipient countries in economic growth, greater efficiency and new consumer products.[37]

It is difficult to reconcile the two statements—one emphasizing employment generation as a goal of development and the other measuring the benefits derived from technology diffusion in terms of increased efficiency and growth rates. As long as U.S. and other foreign businessmen fail to see the contradiction in the two viewpoints, there will be little hope for the voluntary participation of the MNC in the widespread introduction of appropriate technologies designed to help tackle Latin America's enormous un- and underemployment problem.

MNC JOB-CREATING CAPABILITIES

It is hoped that the multinational corporation will soon grasp the significance of the mounting job crisis and perceive its relevance to the corporation's own survival in Latin America. An attractive economic and secure political environment should be a goal of a foreign enterprise, yet it is inconceivable that the number of unemployed can increase unabated without stability being undermined. In this respect, it is certainly in the interest of the foreign firm to put its resources to work in helping to solve the problem. It should also encourage national governments to establish regulations requiring all companies to pursue this end, so that no individual firm is dissuaded from such efforts on account of the competitive disadvantages it might suffer in the short run. Furthermore, MNCs should bring their collective influence to bear on the region's governments to implement a full-employment strategy.

Foreign corporations possess many of the resources that are in short supply in Latin America. These include technical and managerial skills, capital, access to markets, and research and engineering capabilities. With these particular resources at hand, MNCs are in an excellent position to institute managerial and technical training programs, use and develop local suppliers, help create new indigenous industrial systems, and develop products that meet low-income needs.[38]

In the managerial field, international firms can make a significant contribution in the manufacture and export of labor-intensive products. Reliable and quality workers are generally attracted by higher-paying jobs in factories that manufacture in a capital-intensive manner and allow little latitude for error. It is here that expert management is essential and it is to such enterprises that the top mangerial personnel is also drawn. Less qualified managers are more likely to be found in the more labor-intensive, wider-latitude industries where there is more room for error but where, as a consequence, efficiency suffers.[39] If the region's employment problem is to find part of its solution in the more labor-intensive industries, highly qualified managerial talent must be found. Foreign firms and managers appear to be particularly well suited for this role.

The MNC should adapt its production techniques so that they more closely reflect the factor endowments of each locale and should assist domestic enterprises in doing the same. It must recognize that its competitive advantage frequently lies not in its use of capital-intensive technologies, but in its managerial skills, which can render the utilization of labor-intensive methods equally, if not more, profitable. In addition, the MNCs technical abilities can assure the maintenance of high standards of quality in its output, thereby enabling the use of labor-absorbing techniques even in export production.

The international firm can also further the development of local enterprises, as well as national economies, by being selective in its licensing arrangements. It should avoid selling technologies that are inappropriate for local conditions, used for the production of unnecessary items, or inordinately expensive. It is important to educate indigenous firms to the cost structures for R&D and product development, "since many Latin Americans are ignorant of the true cost of technology."[40]

Thus far we have examined the extent to which the multinational corporation has responded to the need and opportunities for employment generation in Latin America and have indicated several areas in which this response can and should be expanded. We need also consider, however, the equally important question of whether the MNC has the managerial and technical flexibility and capability to allow it to make a contribution to the problem's resolution. More specifically, does the foreign firm, even if it is willing, possess the ability to alter its technology to employ greater numbers of the relatively low-wage, low-skilled workers in the Latin American labor force?

There are some who feel that the years of experience that American and European companies have had operating in less developed countries have given them the ability to adapt to these different environments. Mason writes that, through this experience, "a cadre of management and technical personnel has developed," which has a "deeper appreciation of the problems of development including the difficulties of using low level skills . . . ."[41] Similarly, Daniel Margolies claims that "the manager of the plant owned by the multinational corporation has the technical training and experience, plus the experience shared within the organization, so that he is able to organize production in such a way as to optimize the use of low-cost labor."[42]

These opinions, however, are not widely held. A more common view is that expressed by Urquidi:

Foreign capital. . . despite the multiple and repeated hard lessons it has received in its relations with Latin America, is in turn, despite some notable exceptions, lacking in the flexibility necessary to meet the changing mood of the region and the new requirements of development.[43]

Grant sees part of the problem in the infrequency with which most foreign corporate executives have contact with the poorer classes, leaving them virtually unaware of the seriousness of the problem and of the "time bomb ticking away in most developing countries."[44]

Interviews with business leaders tended to support Grant's assessment. Most disclaimed that the MNC has any role to play in job generation except through the promotion of more rapid economic growth and perhaps through the use of local suppliers. The consensus was that the contribution that the U.S. corporation can make to Latin American industrial development is the infusion of American managerial methods and those technologies developed, refined, and in use in the United States. The view commonly expressed was that American companies know little about labor-intensive industries and that most do not possess the managerial flexibility to implement or utilize them.

In its study of MNCs, the National Academy of Sciences articulated similar findings. It found U.S. managers and technicians to be accustomed to high-volume production systems designed in and for the developed countries and to be unfamiliar with other, less highly mechanized techniques. They no longer have any experience with the latter and tend to look upon them as being inferior. Apparently, appropriateness is not a consideration.

Furthermore, the foreign corporation, according to the report, generally lacks familiarity with the cultural and other variables that are prerequisites for an appreciation of the production method best suited for a particular country or region.[45]

Baranson found that large firms are often unwilling to adjust their corporate philosophy and practice to accommodate the needs of their affiliates in developing countries. It takes a special corporate self-image, according to Baranson, to risk investments in the development of new technologies for such different environments, and most firms are not willing to face these long-term uncertainties or the extra innovational effort required.[46]

Mason reports that plant designs and reequipment decisions are usually made through consultation between the manufacturing affiliate overseas and engineers at the U.S. headquarters, allowing the former considerable latitude in making the final selection.[47] He suggests, however, as does Strassmann,[48] that this latitude is largely illusionary, as the options presented to the subsidiaries by U.S.-based engineers are usually limited to a few of the well-known methods used in the developed countries. The problems that can be created by this failure to communicate more appropriate technological alternatives is illustrated by accounts from managers of two U.S. manufacturing subsidiaries in developing countries:[49]

Frequently U.S. engineers will install a machine tool which we can't really use. We are not concerned with cutting down on labor whereas they are. This is not a serious obstacle. It just means that we have to send our people to the U.S. for training so that we can adapt the technology.

And:

In our international operations, we need to get rid of engineers who are committed to current U.S. technology. They have not had enough experience in international operations. Our plant here is too highly automated and difficult to maintain. Also, our equipment is too specialized.

In his 1971 survey of fifty MNCs, Baranson made similar suggestions. Little flexibility was demonstrated by any of the firms, leaving the production techniques in question in most cases unadjusted to the different conditions encountered in the new environment.[50] He finds MNCs, in general, failing to meet the challenges and special needs of the poorer countries in the field of technology and elsewhere. Few of them are capable of adjusting, for, according to Baranson, they are too large and entrenched in their ways to turn themselves around. Because of its lack of flexibility and its general ignorance of cultural variables, as well as the existence of investment environments that favor capital-intensive production, he does not foresee the multinational corporation making a true social contribution to the developing world.

Harry Johnson is equally skeptical about the foreign corporation's capabilities and potential as a development agent when it is left to its own devices:

In concrete terms, reliance on foreign direct investment to promote development can mean highly uneven development. . . . The corporation's concern in establishing branch operations in a particular developing economy is not to promote the development of that economy. . . . It has no commercial interest in diffusing its knowledge to potential local competitors, nor has it any interest in investing more than it has to in acquiring knowledge of local conditions and investigating ways of adapting its own productive knowledge to local factor-price ratios and market conditions. Its purpose is. . . to exploit the existing situation to its own profit by utilization of the knowledge it already possesses. . . .[51]

At a U.N. panel discussion in 1970, members of the international business community objected to being characterized as socially insensitive and expressed the view that foreign firms consisted primarily of "human beings who were concerned with the problems of developing countries" and that these firms "had less to lose by promoting change than be resisting it."[52] Dennison adds that MNCs understand the unemployment problem and are aware of the questions raised about capital-intensive technology. He then goes on, however, to cite the view of Barend A. DeVries that:

. . . it is extremely difficult to conceive of a lasting solution to the employment problem without a rapid growth in the country's own foreign exchange earnings and the availability of mass produced consumer goods. Both of these may . . . be achieved most rapidly by capital-intensive technology and the use of foreign management.[53]

The Council of the Americas, representing 86 percent of the U.S. companies operating in Latin America, expresses a similar opinion. In its 1973 Annual Report, it states that "the essential ingredients of rapid economic development anywhere in the world are skilled manpower, modern technology and large amounts of capital." A like note was sounded at the Council's eighth annual meeting by Fletcher Byrom, Chairman of the Koppers Company. "If living standards are to increase," he claimed, "per capita wealth creation must increase. It is not possible to distribute wealth that has not been created."[54] These views, better than anything else, demonstrate the folly of waiting for the MNC to work for meaningful development in Latin America.

SUMMARY

To date, multinational corporations have rarely attempted to develop and adopt technologies appropriate for the labor-abundant economies of Latin America. In light of government policies that protect markets but not patents, raise the cost of labor and lower that of capital, and in general encourage the use of more "modern" production methods, this is not surprising. In addition, the MNC is strongly influenced by its access to capital abroad and by a number of non-wage-related local labor problems. Some claim, furthermore, that there are limits to the MNC's cultural adaptability and to its technological and managerial flexibility. There is reason to believe, however, that the foreign corporation will manage to overcome these barriers if given the proper incentives. Similarly, governments must take firm action if they are to convince the foreign firm to share its technological capabilities, for it is certainly not in the short-term corporate interest to do so. In light of the negative impact that these companies can have on local economies—in the form of a monopolization of their credit supplies or the displacement of traditional enterprises, for example—and in view of the potential positive impact that their local linkages and demonstration effects can have on the employment situation, strong government policies are all the more imperative.

7 THE ROLE OF LATIN AMERICAN GOVERNMENTS

The national governments of Latin America vary in their approaches to the social and economic development of their respective countries, but they seem to have in common a relative disregard for the problems of un- and underemployment. Although there are many instances of job-creation programs, they usually do not enjoy high priority in the scheme of national economic plans. Other goals, such as economic growth, price stability, and a more favorable balance of payments, relegate employment to a subordinate position—something to be pursued as long as it does not impede the attainment of one or more of the real priorities. Much rhetoric has been heard about creating new jobs; what is required now is comprehensive and committed action. Governments have the necessary tools at their disposal, but so far have lacked the perspective and political will to put them to work.

GENERAL APPROACH TO THE PROBLEM

There still predominates in the region the belief that rapid economic growth is the surest way of eventually including everyone in the development process. Almost three decades of evidence to the contrary have done little to shake this belief. All too often, it must be added, this theory of development has served as an excuse for protecting and advancing the interests of the powerful at the expense of the poor. Even those political leaders who might choose an alternate route are usually limited in their action by strong, favored groups such as large industrialists and the more highly paid workers in the modern sector. The support given to capital-intensive, large-scale enterprises has strengthened the hand of these groups in maintaining the system as is.

As a result of these factors, most Latin American governments have continued their support of these favored few. Foreign exchange rates have generally been too high, the price of domestic capital has usually been kept artificially low, the larger industrialists have been favored in capital rationing, inefficient operations have been protected in the name of import substitution, labor unions and the pay of their members have been bolstered by the populist leaders of the continent, and in some cases even payroll taxes have been levied. In short, the policy record in Latin America has shown, and continues to show, a subsidization of large capital interests and a disregard for the unemployed of the region.

This capital-intensive approach has been perpetuated in other ways, as well. Vernon discusses the internal role of foreign-owned firms, but reasons that, regardless of their input,

... these [less developed] countries are bound to rely heavily on the technology, the markets, and even the consumption norms of outside nations. The tie is particularly strong because so-called modernizing attitudes, such as the desire for more education, growth, and choice, as well as the willingness to save, are commonly found closely linked with a desire for "modern" goods. If the economy is small, the reliance is likely to be great; if the economy is committed to rapid growth, the reliance may be greater still.[1]

The ILO found that governments, as well as consumers, ". . . often, in effect, encourage the tendency toward capital-intensive methods by their preference for standardized products, rapidly produced by large-scale industry." Furthermore, these changes in demand are not completely spontaneous but, rather, induced by mass advertising, while hand-made traditional goods receive no such advantage.[2]

The real priorities of the respective governments of the region were reflected by their representatives at the CACTAL (Conference on the Application of Science and Technology to Latin American Development) meetings in 1972 in Brasilia. Although statements were made to the effect that adaptations should be made in imported technology so as to take into account employment policies, the CACTAL consensus, not surprisingly, gave emphasis to a quite different matter. "Scientific and technological development," it stated, "should aim at efficient modernization of the production system [and] should give preferential attention . . . to development of the most dynamic sectors of the economy that make intensive use of advanced technologies."[3]

In the end, CACTAL revealed its top priority—economic growth. A strategy of technological development and employment promotion should, in the words of its consensus, "prevent measures designed to increase employment through restrictions on the use of capital-intensive technologies that might well result in less economic growth by damaging the competitive position and potential of important productive sectors and, therefore, the future demand for workers." This growth-means-jobs philosophy is accompanied as usual by the view that jobs should be generated in the construction, public works, services, and agricultural sectors.[4] The participants at CACTAL clearly demonstrated their lack of commitment to the creation of new employment opportunities in the manufacturing sector.

It is not surprising, therefore, that Latin American governments have shown little interest in pressuring foreign companies to adopt more labor-absorbing production techniques. Even those countries, such as Brazil and and the Andean Group nations, which in recent years have improved their bargaining positions vis-à-vis the MNC, have not utilized their increased leverage to induce concessions in this area. Yet as governments are forced to respond to changing social and economic realities in their countries, the nature of their negotiating demands could change as well. As they give greater attention to the questions of mass poverty and massive unemployment, a conflict could well develop between national employment goals and what the MNC perceives as its corporate interests. The ensuing confrontation would center around such issues as the choice, development, and transfer of appropriate technologies, changes in product mix and demand patterns, and other MNC policies that are inconsistent with the relative factor scarcities and availabilities of the poor countries.[5]

Grant feels that MNCs will increasingly be asked to justify the technology they use in developing countries, in view of the deepening employment crisis. He contends that ". . . these countries will place a particularly high premium on foreign investments which promise to provide, directly or indirectly, significant added employment. If the developed countries encourage—or at least permit—the current trend toward the internationalizing of production that is by nature labor-intensive, the image of foreign investment should be enhanced."[6]

On the other hand, some American businessmen active in Latin America have noted that, in negotiations, the governments of the region will generally sell out on the point of employment, if they broach the subject at all. Bradford argues that "despite the rising force of nationalism in Latin America and the increasing importance of employment, which would seem to focus greater attention on labor-using techniques, the dynamic, high-technology industries in which the U.S. has particular prowess, are vital to future growth, employment and trade prospects in Latin America."[7] While this evaluation of the needs of the region is subject to serious dispute, there is little doubt that most of the political leaders of Latin America share similar beliefs. Under these circumstances, Bradford is most probably accurate in claiming that the dynamic industries will generally remain open to foreign investment:

Despite what has to be considered a mammoth employment problem looming in the years ahead, the opportunities open for investment in industry are not likely to be affected by the impact of this problem on development policy. . . . Radical departures in development strategies, stressing labor-intensive industries and public works to the exclusion of the dynamic industries, are not likely to occur. The more consciousness there is of the employment question as a long-run problem, the more Latin American governments will be seeking technology and investment resources to advance modern industry.[8]

As there has been throughout the region an emphasis on rapid export expansion as a means of spurring economic development, many countries feel that they need these foreign inputs in order to be able to compete in world markets. Although much of their production destined for developed countries has indeed been of a capital-intensive nature, some labor-intensive engineering products are sold there as well. Baranson strikes a note of optimism when he suggests that export promotion, employment generation, and the role of the MNC may all be compatible in these countries:

The shifting emphases in industrialization strategies toward outward-oriented export industries and toward a more discreet range of import-substitution industries, including more consumer products for low-income groups, have far-reaching implications for U.S.-based MNCs. This is where they have continued interest in penetrating LDC markets and in utilizing offshore manufacturing sites with low-wage labor in order to compete in world markets.[9]

As a general rule, however, Latin American governments have accepted—in fact, usually promoted—MNC capital-intensive production for both domestic and foreign markets.

NATIONAL POLICIES

There is no better illustration of the emphasis upon capital-intensive production in Latin America than the current Brazilian development model. While liberal foreign investment laws have helped to attract a heavy flow of outside money and technology, Brazil is now in a strong position to make increasing demands upon foreign companies. Yet these demands will clearly focus on breaking down the investment package, rather than on pressuring the MNC to increase its rate of job creation.

The 1972–74 Brazilian National Development Plan called for the development of new industrial sectors with a high technological content—such as the chemical industry, nonferrous metals, electronics, aeronautics, and naval construction—as well as the consolidation of the "Basic Industries," which include iron and steel, capital goods, construction, and nonmetallic minerals. Chemicals, iron and steel, electronics, and some aspects of the aeronautics industry received priority under the heading of "High Technological Content Industries."[10] Major components in the 13.9 percent growth in industrial output in 1972 were steel ingots, chemicals and petrochemicals, motor vehicles, cement, and electricity.[11] The first two of these industries were projected to experience the most rapid growth in production through 1975.

In a 1971 publication, Business International Corporation referred to the Brazilian government's "Current List of Basic Industries," citing the priority that had been assigned to them and adding that "the welcome mat is out to investors in these industries. . . ."[12] Leading Brazilian cabinet members have further defined the role of foreign investment in their economy. In November 1972, the finance minister, Antônio Delfim Neto, stated that foreign capital was still essential to the development of Brazil, as these funds were needed to ensure a 9 to 10 percent growth rate over the next few years.[13] Planning Minister João Paulo dos Reis Velloso has explained that "foreign investment is frequently expected to play a pioneering and innovating role, via the introduction of new products and of new sectors—which, by the way, are normally among the most dynamic industrial branches. . . " and that MNCs can make a contribution "through the increase in the technological content of Brazilian industrial production. . . ."[14]

The National Development Plan declared that "foreign enterprises should orient their investments mainly towards areas of more sophisticated technology, where the transfer of modern technology and modern management methods to this country becomes relevant."[15] In this way, Brazil will be better capable of competing in world markets. According to Reis Velloso, MNCs can support Brazil's export drive "through understanding with the parent companies, allowing participation of Brazilian subsidiaries in external markets."[16]

The Development Plan did recognize the problems of overt unemployment and underemployment in the Brazilian economy. Noting that during the 1950s the annual employment increase in the secondary sector was only 2.3 percent despite an industrial production growth of 9 percent, the plan set out employment targets for the early 1970s. GNP growth was programmed at between 8 and 10 percent, contingent upon the increase in employment of a yearly average of 3.1 percent.[17] At the beginning of this decade, new jobs were being created at a rate of 2.8 percent annually, which was somewhat below the rate of population increase.

Delfim Neto stated in 1972 that the government clearly recognized the problem of severe income inequality in the country and would not approve "any measure which goes against the redistribution of income." He claimed that, while the minimum wage was doubled in 1964, increases have since been moderated so as to avoid inducing the use of more capital-intensive methods in industry.[18] The Development Plan suggested shifting some of the tax burden from company payrolls to sales value. In addition, emphasis was placed upon manpower training, as a reaction to the 6 percent annual increase in urban population during the 1960s. In an attempt to stem migration from the country's Northeast, the government introduced a new program in December 1972 for the economic development of the region. The National Economic Development Bank (BNDE) was directed to make available additional investment funds on top of those attracted by SUDENE's "34/18" reinvestment system which, by and large, has resulted in investments of a capital-intensive nature. SUDENE (Superintendency for the Development of the Northeast) and BNDE monitor each project jointly in order to ensure that it increases job opportunities rather than reducing them through greater automation.[19]

One does not have to go much further than the National Development Plan itself, however, to see the basic contradictions between the government's stated objectives in employment generation and its plans in other areas. It should not go unnoticed, for example, that the area of employment is the final one covered by the plan. Mahbub ul Haq has recently observed that

... looking at the national plans of the developing countries, it was obvious that employment was often a secondary, not a primary, objective of planning. It was generally added as an afterthought to the growth target in GNP but very poorly integrated in the framework of planning. Recalling my own experience with the formulation of Pakistan's five-year plans—and I ought to know—the chapter on employment strategy was always added at the end, to round off the plans and make them look complete and respectable, and was hardly an integral part of the growth strategy or policy framework.[20]

Although the Brazilian plan expressed a need for greater "internal technological elaboration," the creation of "national models and processes," and a "better utilization of the country's comparative advantages with respect to production costs,"[21] priority was still given to areas of advanced technology. While industry in the Northeast should use less capital-intensive production techniques than that in the Center-South, according to the plan, this "should not impair the viability of implemented projects, whose technology must allow competition vis-á-vis the Center-South."[22] Another somewhat ambiguous comment is also found in the plan's section on employment. "The national development objective," it states, "is not purely and simply to achieve the full employment of the available manpower, because it can coexist even with complete stagnation or with a low GNP growth."[23] It can be assumed that a slow GNP growth rate, in the Brazilian view, is anything under 8 percent.

Some other interesting observations are also made in the employment chapter. For example, industrial employment expansion was projected at an annual rate of 4.1 percent through 1974, although this sector provided new jobs at a rate of 5.7 percent a year during the past decade. The explanation given for this expected decline, which includes a one percent drop in job opportunities in processing industries, was that such high growth rates in the secondary sector would tend to aggravate the employment problems of the urban areas. It is interesting that no reference is made within this context to the possibilities of industrial growth in rural areas. It should also be noted that emphasis was again placed upon the construction and construction materials industries for manpower absorption within the industrial sector.[24]

As far as factor prices are concerned, the plan called for a continuation of the policy that progressively reduced interest rates and raised real average wages. Policies for cheaper capital were designed "in order to transfer the so obtained cost reductions to the productive system." Wage rate policy was designed to ensure that the worker's pay progressively increases "in real terms, proportionally to the overall productivity gains," despite the fact that these gains are largely brought about through increased mechanization. No comment was made about the possibility of higher wages inducing more capital-intensive production methods.

The British press has spelled out quite clearly that which can be inferred from the Brazilian plan. *The Economist's* Intelligence Unit needed to turn only to Delfim Neto's own phrase, *"crescer é concentrar"* ("to grow is to concentrate"), to demonstrate the government's intent of achieving rapid growth in developed regions at the expense of removing regional disparities. *The Economist* added that an "all-around improvement in the short term can be achieved only if investment is directed to labour-intensive rather than capital-intensive projects; and so far, by and large, it has gone to the latter."[25]

As part of a *Financial Times* survey of Brazil in October 1972, Emanuel de Kadt discussed the problem of income distribution. It is worth quoting de Kadt at length:

The whole thrust of government policy is towards further developing those parts of the country (and of the economy) that are already more advanced, and towards encouraging the integration of Brazil's urban-industrial sector (and its modern service sector) into the international economic system, whose standards of technology and productivity are set in the industrialized countries of the Northern Hemisphere. Little attention is apparently paid to the problems of unemployment and underemployment, on which the Brazilian government significantly publishes no meaningful data. The vast rural work force, and here one is talking about some 13 m. people plus dependents, is forgotten in these policies, and in case someone argues that migration to the towns will solve all that, it should be remembered that the bloated urban "service sector" in the labour force statistics already contains literally millions of people on the verge of starvation.

Nor does the type of industrial growth pursued give much hope to these people. No effort is apparently going into the stimulation of industries using labour-intensive production methods. "Nothing but the best for Brazil," is surely nonsense. While some branches of manufacturing do need to use the latest available technology if they are to compete successfully in the international market, many goods made with "intermediate" technologies can also be sold abroad. Moreover, this vast new industrial complex is inappropriate for producing the kinds of products desperately needed by those who so far have hardly any purchasing power. For them, Brazil's growth pattern seems to hold little in store.

A good indication is that the output of industries producing semi-durable consumer goods, such as textiles, footwear, or clothing, has stagnated between 1964 and 1970; in contrast in the electrical and electronic industries output rose by 113 percent and the car industry pushed its production up by a staggering 143 percent. And in professional circles the question is now being raised whether it will not become increasingly difficult for structural reasons to tackle the extreme inequalities once a growing share of total wages is generated in industries producing for high income groups.[26]

Furthermore, it is de Kadt's observation that Brazil "has been open to foreign investment without any regard for the types of technology imported or their appropriateness to creating employment for the millions effectively left out of the economy."[27] Even recent government plans for foreign investment in the Northeast have emphasized the importation of complete industrial plants.[28] Although internal debate over alternative development strategies has increased, Brazil remains committed to an export-led growth based upon the utilization of modern, capital-intensive technologies. This is reflected in the government's industrial development strategy for 1975-79, which emphasizes the further development of the capital goods and electronics industries, the execution of sophisticated and large-scale projects to expand the exportation of manufactures, and industrial R, D &E concentrated on high-technology industries.

The Andean Pact countries, as a group, have adopted much more restrictive foreign investment rules than has their giant neighbor. Even so, the restrictions appear to have very little to do with employment generation. While it is encouraging that their pact calls for the screening of imported technology and requires member governments to give preference to products developed from local technology, no mention of employment is made in this regard. In fact, only once in the Andean Agreement of Subregional Integration is the issue referred to at all.

The role reserved for the MNC is that of an engine for economic growth. In this regard, the Andean Group seeks to channel foreign investment toward specific goals, including technological growth and market expansion. Because MNCs develop, transfer, and use sophisticated production techniques, they are seen as a major source of R&D, labor training, and most importantly, a technology that can be transferred to local industrialists. If foreign companies can be forced to share their technological advances, as well as direct their investment into key industrial sectors, Andean Group members feel that the effect will be an eventual modernization of their entire production systems.[29] The situation this presages is one of national manufacturing sectors built upon complex machinery and skilled labor, while urban unemployment continues to grow unabated.

Of all the Andean countries, Colombia has most frequently been the subject of recent employment studies. They reveal that since 1962 there has been a significant decline in the rate of growth in manufacturing employment in the country after a surge of expansion between 1958 and 1962. The ILO has found that in the industrial sector the greatest priority has been given to the expansion of the cement, machinery, petrochemical, automobile, pharmaceutical, printing, electronics, and steel industries, with particular emphasis placed upon the promotion of the capital goods industries. Although industry is still dominated by consumer-goods production, the share of total industrial production held by capital goods has risen sharply since 1950. An industrial strategy which, as a matter of policy, increasingly emphasizes investment in these areas may be successful in improving the balance-of-payments situation, but at the same time frequently requires a rising investment outlay for each new job created. Employment generation apparently has not been given much consideration in these new investment decisions.[30]

The ILO employment report, prepared by a team headed by Dudley Seers, notes that decisions taken in Colombia in recent years reflect systematic biases against labor-intensive and toward more capital-intensive production techniques and concludes that this accounts in large part for the slow growth of employment in the industrial sector. It goes on to explain some of the biases built into the system:

In Colombia, the implications of technological policy for industry taking account of the employment aspects, and the need to use the available factors of production in a rational way, has received up to now very little attention from either government or the private sector. It has been widely assumed that all imports of machinery were a good thing for the economy, and that the adoption of any modern technique was desirable. In consequence, imports of machinery have tended to receive preferential treatment in the tariff structure and in the granting of import permits, without due consideration to their employment implications. If to this is added the effect of periodic exchange over-valuation, the relatively low interest rates, and the easier access to credit enjoyed by large modern companies using capital-intensive techniques, we have a composite picture which, besides discouraging the development of a local capital goods industry, tends to make it easy and cheap to buy machinery.[31]

Another set of observers of the Colombian scene[32] has focused upon the formulators of many of these decisions—the modern political elite, composed of politicians and *técnicos* operating within the traditional political parties. This modernizing group has stressed socioeconomic "efficiency" rather than the redistribution of wealth and the creation of additional job opportunities. An examination of policies and leaders at the beginning of this decade led these observers to conclude that

... the policies ... being used are not viable over the long run. Population will grow and migrate to the cities looking for work. A technical bureaucracy with an ideological interest in "efficiency" will continue to evolve, and the conflicts of interest latent in the present system will become increasingly apparent.[33]

Such attitudes and biases presented major obstacles to the immediate implementation of the full-employment strategy designed by the Seers team in 1970. The team was invited back for a follow-up mission in the spring of 1973, but the government of Misael Pastrana Borrero did little in way of implementing its basic recommendations. Some critics have suggested that the report has been used solely for political purposes, but Seers has remained sanguine that the report will ultimately yield beneficial results.

In fact, the present administration of President Alfonso López Michelsen has been more predisposed than its predecessors to follow the type of economic and social policies that are in line with the study's recommendations. Most encouraging is the fact that Jorge Mendez Munévar, a key member of the Seers team, presently holds the important position of director of the Institute of Industrial Development. Since the beginning of the new administration in 1974, the government has demonstrated an active interest in employment-generating programs, including the provision of efficient credit facilities for small- and medium-sized industry. Given the current precarious state of the Colombian economy, however, López Michelsen is operating from a position of weakness when he encounters congressional and other opposition to such social legislation.

In Venezuela, a stronger economic situation enables President Carlos Andrés Pérez to handle more effectively opposition to his social reforms. He and his progressive planning minister, Gumersindo Rodriguez, have shown concern for the 600,000 un- and underemployed of their country, but some of the measures taken to date have been of questionable value. Many of these have been aimed at creating jobs in a service sector that is already overburdened. Others, such as new labor regulations that have increased job security and raised the minimum wage, reflect social concern but will also have negative effects on employment in the industrial sector. Furthermore, the government, despite having shown some interest in alternative technologies, has continued to favor capital-intensive investment, both domestic and foreign. For example, an additional $5 billion will be invested in the state-owned steel plant in Ciudad Guayana, but only 7,000 new jobs will be created over four years.

Elsewhere in the Andean region, Chile has also continued to encourage capital-intensive industrial investment. A United Nations study group[34] has identified this proclivity as a major cause of unemployment and has recommended that measures be adopted to reduce the artificially high price of labor with respect to the price of capital. Suggestions to this end include the financing of the social security system in such a way that the tax burden falls more heavily upon the use of capital rather than that of labor. (A similar study of Costa Rica also emphasized the need for a realignment of factor prices.[35]) Peru, on the other hand, appears to be interested in increasing employment in the manufacturing sector, if only to the extent of considering the magnitude of job creation—measured by both the number of employees and the size of the company's payroll—when screening foreign investments.[36]

Mexico provides an example of a country where rapid economic growth has been accompanied by an equally rapid growth in underemployment and where official rhetoric concerning the creation of more employment opportunities has not been matched by effective action. This is not to deny the interest of the government of President Luis Echeverría Alvarez in the welfare of the poor, particularly the rural poor. But despite the government's efforts to spread employment opportunities more evenly throughout the country, it has been relying upon industrial expansion rather than changes in production technologies to provide more jobs in that sector. So far there has not been much progress toward the achievement of national industrial employment targets for 1976.

National intermediate-goods industries, such as chemicals, nonmetallic minerals, and iron and steel, have grown quite rapidly. The same is true of the consumer-goods industry, as an effort has been made to replace imported consumer goods with domestic products. For example, the government has stipulated that at least 60 percent of the components for the Mexican motor industry (which is almost entirely foreign controlled) must be nationally made. Employment-generating effects, however, have been disappointing. It has been suggested by Morgan, in fact, that one result of these policies has been a further growth in structural unemployment.[37] Grant points more specifically to the bias contained in the policies that encourage the use of labor-saving production techniques.[38]

To date, MNCs in Mexico have favored capital-intensive investment. Furthermore, the nature of the incentives in the 1973 Foreign Investment Law for employment of greater numbers of workers in new factories may reflect more an interest in attracting investment than a concern about unemployment. Although it is true that foreign capital must complement rather than replace Mexican capital and that foreign firms must bring in new rather than "outdated" technology, such provisions can only lead to further capital-intensive foreign investment. The new national law on the transfer of technology makes repeated reference to the need for both access to the most modern foreign technology and the promotion of the country's own technological development, but there is no mention of the need for a type of technology that would increase employment.[39] This is consistent with an opinion expressed by the Mexican government in a document submitted at the CACTAL meetings. Its official position was that ". . . the possibilities of adopting labor-intensive and capital-saving technologies that are also efficient and in keeping with productivity standards are very few and very often their adoption may endanger the ability to compete in international markets."[40]

Mexico will remain for the foreseeable future one of the most attractive markets for foreign investment in Latin America. It is taking advantage of this situation to extract from MNCs certain concessions in areas such as technology, exporting, local purchase, and plant location. It expects these companies to exhibit a greater sense of social responsibility, but there is little indication that an increased role in direct employment creation falls under this general rubric.

Employment generation in Latin America overall has not been a primary goal of its policy-makers. It has been the subject of much discussion and of many political statements, but rarely the object of effective action. In isolated cases, governments have taken limited action in this area, but they have done little to promote labor-intensive industrial technology. Nor does it seem likely that MNCs will be pressured by host governments to make employment-generating technological adaptations. Demands upon foreign firms for local control, local purchasing, exporting, and assistance in upgrading domestic technological capabilities will increase, but the governments of the region do not appear ready, or particularly motivated, to pressure these companies in the area of direct job creation per se.

RECOMMENDATIONS FOR GOVERNMENT POLICY

On the assumption, however, that the day must soon come when many of the governments of Latin America will be forced to recognize employment as a true priority area, it is important to spell out the available policy alternatives for inducing the use of more labor-intensive production methods in the manufacturing sector. Of particular interest here are those policies that could be effective in eliciting a positive response from foreign investors. Grant, among others, feels that the creation of a policy environment conducive to labor-intensive profitability is clearly the single most important change necessary for the promotion of MNC industrial labor-intensivity. He points to successful policy implementation by Korea and Taiwan and advises that MNCs be ready to adapt in Latin America within a decade.

The ILO report on Colombia considers the selection of such policies and the extent of their use. It suggests that a "government might choose to bias decisions deliberately in favour of labour-intensive techniques—not just eliminate the biases in the other direction." Once the oversimplified view that income distribution must follow output maximization is discarded, writing new rules of the game becomes a risky undertaking. Accordingly, "it is not easy," the report concludes, "to suggest how far the decision makers should venture into such unchartered territory, though this is the direction in which a new emphasis on unemployment and on relieving poverty will lead. There is certainly a case for techniques which, though 'socially' more costly, raise employment and the incomes of the poor."[41]

Developing countries have a variety of policy instruments at their disposal with which they can exert influence over the choice of production techniques in their industrial sectors, in general, and by multinational enterprises, in particular. An indirect approach encompasses the implementation of a package of measures designed to modify the local economic environment so as to induce the selection of more labor-intensive technologies by foreign, as well as domestic, firms. A more direct approach, applicable to MNCs alone, involves the screening of foreign investment and the stipulation of relevant terms of entry in the original investment contract.

Indirect measures must include the realignment of distorted factor prices, which are a principal cause of excessive capital-intensity in Latin

American industry. While it is necessary to deal with engineering and business biases, as well as other factors that promote the utilization of labor-saving methods, the rectification of these prices alone would go a long way toward matching the choice of technologies with the relative factor scarcities of a nation. Given this need, efforts must be focused upon identifying the steps that can be taken to lower the cost of labor and raise that of capital.

Some recommendations are made below. With respect to labor, it is important to restate that its price involves much more than simply direct wages. There are also possible training expenses, fringe benefits, taxes upon labor use, restrictive labor laws, strikes, difficulties in management, and so forth. Governments must help minimize some of these costs in order to encourage an expanded use of labor.

1. *Wages:* holding down wages in the modern sector can often be difficult for political reasons, but low-paid labor could be subsidized and taxes placed on the cost of overtime labor and the use of skilled workers; or a general wage subsidy could be effective.

2. *Payroll taxes:* it is recommended that payroll taxes be eliminated where in effect and a reverse payroll tax be implemented, with tax concessions based upon the number of employees, rather than on the value of investment.

3. *Social security, unemployment compensation, and other insurance schemes:* the current system of financing these services is linked to the level of wage payments whereas, they could be based at least in part upon the book value of the plant and equipment.

4. *Training expenses:* generous write-offs could be permitted or other incentives offered for expenditures made on task-specific, as opposed to industry-specific, training, which would develop skills usable in a number of industries.

5. *Labor laws:* there must be a modification of laws relating to women (particularly the hours a woman can work), overtime (to encourage the use of two or even three shifts), and firing of employees (although jobs may be preserved under present restrictive systems, as mechanization progresses restrictive laws influence original investment decisions toward greater capital-intensivity).

At the same time, the price of capital must be altered. The raising of interest rates per se would probably have very little effect upon MNCs, as they make extensive use of their external sources of funding when making their original investment. Because the price of capital generally does not reflect its true scarcity in Latin America, however, a certain amount of rationing must be done by the banks. Not surprisingly, there is a tendency to make loans to the larger firms and the best credit risks, which include MNCs. Under such circumstances, small local firms are placed at an even greater disadvantage. For this reason and for reasons of promoting the use of labor-intensive technology, some of the following steps should be taken by governments in order to raise the cost of capital.

1. *Interest rates:* allow them to gradually rise to reflect the true scarcity of capital, making adjustments for high rates of inflation.

2. *Exchange rates:* as most Latin American currencies are overvalued and machinery and other imports are thus underpriced, devaluations are in order; systems of multiple exchange rates that favor the purchase of foreign capital goods must also be changed.

3. *Method of depreciation:* systems of accelerated depreciation—often permitted in order to attract foreign investment—should be changed because they reinforce the bias toward capital-intensivity.

4. *Investment and fiscal policy:* a tax could be levied on new fixed capital investment, while tax incentives to reinvest profits should be conditional upon the use of labor-intensive technology.

5. *Import duties:* tariffs on heavy machinery are often relatively low and should be kept at least as high as those placed on other imports.

Another important factor contributing to capital-intensive and inefficient production in many Latin American countries has been policies of *import substitution.* Originally designed to protect infant domestic industries by limiting competitive imports, these policies have also come to protect established local firms, as well as MNCs. In fact, many corporations, restricted in their sales to particular foreign markets, have set up plants within those countries to circumvent their prohibitive tariff barriers. Once established, they need not be particularly cost-conscious, as they are not forced to be price-competitive. The result has been the importation of foreign machinery without regard to local factor prices, even in distorted form. It is clear then that one way of helping to bring about less capital-intensive production is to extend less protection to these industries, exposing them to the winds of competition. Some countries have already begun to do this, though for purposes other than generating employment.

Latin American governments can also stimulate more labor-intensive production by soliciting the help of MNCs in R, D & E efforts directed toward the development of appropriate technologies. In this area, the following steps should be given serious consideration.

1. *Write-offs for R, D & E:* generous write-offs for R, D & E expenditures should be permitted, provided the work is directed toward the development of more labor-intensive technologies.

2. *Fiscal incentives:* outlays by MNCs could be matched by governments in order to encourage more extensive and appropriate R, D & E; Canada, Australia, and Israel have employed policies of this type.[42]

3. *Educational policy:* the government should attempt to form a corps of creative scientists and engineers with the assistance of MNCs where possible; the availability of such personnel would remove one of the obstacles to the local development of appropriate technologies by MNCs.

4. *Patent laws:* national governments should strictly enforce patent laws in order to provide increased protection of local R, D & E and encourage greater activity in this area.

5. *Institutional integration:* there should be greater cooperation among MNCs, domestic private industry, universities, and research institutes, both public and private.

6. *Protectionism:* the removal of protection from outside competition may force some MNCs to undertake more local, appropriate R, D & E in an effort to stay competitive.

7. *Contract stipulations:* when negotiating the original investment, the MNC should be required to invest a certain percentage of its pretax profits in locally based R, D & E and to make a reasonable contribution toward process and product innovation.

Before discussing other possible contract stipulations, additional government measures deserve attention. It is necessary, as stated earlier, for national governments to recognize the costs that attend biases toward capital-intensive investment on the part of businessmen, economists, engineers, and local government officials. In order to eliminate these biases, professional education must be reoriented to emphasize the differences between local socioeconomic needs and conditions and those of the developed countries. The expansion and reorientation of professional education in Latin American countries would lessen the reliance upon American and European professional schools, while producing more socially sensitive industrialists and policy-makers at home.

Of equal importance is the need to increase awareness of the existence of the range of technological alternatives available in each industry. To this end, national or regional centers should be established to gather and disseminate information about more appropriate, labor-intensive technologies. Governments can then encourage their utilization by purchasing a large proportion of their goods from those firms that produce most labor-intensively.

These measures alone, however, may not be sufficient to induce foreign corporations to change their production methods. Accordingly, national boards should screen and evaluate all foreign investment proposals on the basis of, among other things, the appropriateness of the technological content and the potential contribution of the investment to local job creation. Investment contracts should then stipulate that a particular technology be utilized or that a certain minimum number of workers be employed by the MNC; local content requirements should also be prescribed where not already in effect. Such a direct approach by host countries can be most effective, according to some company executives, when the right economic environment is created and the proper incentives are offered. In order to ensure employment maximization, as well as a continued flow of foreign capital, both these direct and indirect approaches must be utilized.

THE MNC RESPONSE

A great many corporate managers feel, however, that Latin American governments will not exert maximum pressure on the MNC, particularly for the purpose of employment generation. A sampling of opinion from among executives of United States-based companies operating in the region reveals a fairly common theme. Host governments will not make "unreasonable" demands upon the MNC, it is argued, for fear of losing the corporation and the benefits it brings to the local economy. And should such pressure be applied, the contention is that the MNC would indeed leave for a more agreeable investment site. One executive stated that if his firm's costs were to be forced upward as a result of such demands without a commensurate rise in productivity, it would be forced to terminate its operations. He emphasized that his company is "not married to Latin America." Another member of the international business community echoed similar sentiments when he scoffingly pointed out that the loss of a market the size of Ecuador's, for example, would hardly constitute a critical blow to any large corporation.

Such threats have been shown by experience, however, to represent far more bark than bite. In Mexico and elsewhere in Latin America—most recently and notably in the Andean Group countries—more stringent requirements imposed by governments on foreign corporations have not been followed by total divestment. A few years ago, the Council of the Americas and other business interests warned that an Andean Group code calling for the progressive transfer of majority interest of MNCs to national stockholders over a ten- to fifteen-year period would mean the virtual end of foreign investment in its member countries. Today Peru, for one, is on the road to fully implementing this policy, yet U.S. investment in manufacturing facilities there appears to be increasing after falling off during the early 1970s.[43] Chrysler, which at one time possessed 50 percent of the Peruvian automotive market, found that it could live with a law that would in time turn over half its stock to its employees. "Who can see 10 years in the future?" queried a company spokesman. "Things will work themselves out."[44]

While the Peruvian situation may leave foreign investors elsewhere in Latin America somewhat apprehensive, in general they do not envisage the need to leave Latin America altogether. It is their contention that, if a particular government were to exert greater pressure upon a foreign firm, the company could find another country in which it could operate more freely. But is this a realistic assumption? Current evidence suggests that nearly all Latin American governments are or will be increasing their demands on MNCs in one form or another, although not necessarily in the employment area.[45] Furthermore, companies cannot remain competitive if they continually shift their manufacturing operations from country to country, leaving behind investments in physical facilities and trained personnel. To think otherwise, according to Ambassador Harald B. Malmgren, former Deputy Special Representative to the President for Trade Negotiations, is to misunderstand business realities. "As a practical matter, most corporations make commitments for the long-term (10 to 20 years) and do not intend to move often."[46]

Moreover, the very factors that sent U.S. corporations overseas originally still act to dissuade them from withdrawing from particular countries that continue to meet their needs. In some cases, vital resources can be found only in a limited location. Certain markets may be essential because of their size or because of the nature of the product being sold. At times, the only access to such markets is through the establishment of manufacturing facilities on the spot. Other countries are important for their location because of extensive exportation to the U.S. and other foreign markets. Others offer the MNC attractive tax-evasion opportunities.

United States corporations will also have to meet the challenge of the Europeans and the Japanese, whose investments in Latin America have grown rapidly over the past several years and who are often more willing and able to accept the new arrangements imposed upon them. Japanese direct investments, which between 1951 and 1967 totalled less than $375 million,[47] have since increased by more than $2 billion, and in Brazil alone the figure today is well over $1 billion. At the same time, indications are that Japanese investors provide more employment per dollar invested in developing countries than do their American counterparts.[48] This is not surprising in light of Japan's own history of industrial development, which had its basis in the development, adaptation, and use of labor-intensive and small-scale technologies. This experience makes the Japanese especially well suited to efficiently employ unskilled workers in Latin America, where labor is similarly abundant and relatively inexpensive.

This capability gives the Japanese, as well as some European investors, a competitive advantage over U.S. corporations and a greater flexibility in responding to host country requirements. Even an organization so closely identified with U.S. overseas business interests as the Council of the Americas has acknowledged the significant effect that this will have on the bargaining position of the U.S. company. A council spokesman conceded that "the growth of multinational firms in the European Economic Community and Japan that can compete effectively with U.S. multinational corporations. . . provides the Latin states with greater negotiating power in their movement toward greater economic independence and control."[49]

This relative increase in bargaining strength is also a consequence of the rapidly increasing knowledge and skill in the negotiating process of many of the region's governments. A growing awareness of the investment alternatives open to the MNC increases a government's leverage and its ability to play off one firm against another. What took decades to learn and implement in the extractive sector is currently becoming far more quickly understood by decision-makers in the manufacturing sector. This knowledge is not yet widely possessed, however, and thus in many countries the foreign corporation will continue to hold the upper hand in negotiations for some time to come. This is particularly true in the area of technological development and transfer. The MNC will resist all attempts by Latin American governments to elicit a contribution to the upgrading of the technological base of its domestic industry, for it is not in the self-perceived corporate interest to restructure and share this know-how.

For the foreseeable future, therefore, those governments that remain in a weak bargaining position might be well advised, in the opinion of Baranson, to establish a much more extensive set of contractual arrangements with small- and medium-sized foreign firms. These are usually more adaptive in their technology and more flexible about sharing it because of the relatively few overseas investment alternatives available to them. Meanwhile, host governments throughout the region should concentrate on sharpening their negotiating skills, and in cases in which sufficient bargaining strength has been attained, should pressure even the large corporations to develop, employ, and share more appropriate, labor-absorbing industrial technologies.

SUMMARY

Given the inability or unwillingness of foreign corporations to recognize that more employment-generating production in Latin America is in their own long-term interests, it is the responsibility of the region's governments to implement policies that would elicit a greater contribution in this area. The latter must create the right economic and policy environments and offer the proper incentives, as well as closely screen foreign investment proposals and make the relevant stipulations in investment contracts. Unfortunately, most governments also do not seem to perceive the importance of reorienting policies so as to substantially expand the number of job opportunities in the industrial sector. It is unrealistic to expect MNCs, given their short-term corporate interests, to become more socially responsible in an area in which host governments themselves have displayed little active interest. On the other hand, it is equally unrealistic for both parties to ignore the growing social tensions inherent in a situation of rapidly expanding urban unemployment. Governments will be the first to be forced to respond to these needs and the dangers they present to their own survival. In turn, they should not be afraid to use their improving bargaining positions to pressure the MNC into participating in employment programs, for, despite their claims to the contrary, it is usually in the interest of these corporations to remain in these countries.

8 SUMMARY AND CONCLUSIONS

Latin America today is faced with a critical and steadily worsening employment problem. Increasingly rapid population growth, particularly over the past thirty years, has swelled the ranks of the labor force as each generation comes of working age. Meanwhile, the rate of new job creation has stagnated. The result has been some of the highest un- and underemployment rates in the world, in both the urban and rural sectors. Estimates of open unemployment begin at 10 percent of the region's labor force and rates of combined un- and underemployment range as high as 50 percent in some countries.

There are few indications that there is much if any relief ahead. Even if it were possible to immediately curtail increases in national populations—currently running at rates above 3 percent in most Latin American countries—the next generation's labor force has already been born. The problem is further complicated by large-scale migrations by underemployed rural workers to urban areas in a usually futile search for more viable employment opportunities.

This calls for a rethinking of development strategies. Efforts concentrated on increasing economic growth rates have enriched some but have left millions unemployed and entire segments of society worse off than ever. The general inability or refusal within Latin America to effectively use fiscal policy to distribute income more equitably points to the importance of increased job creation as a nonviolent alternative to effect such a redistribution. It is imperative that the region's governments no longer follow the growth models of the already developed countries but rather implement policies that utilize the area's most abundant resource and its potentially greatest asset—its labor force. Consequent benefits may range from a shift in demand toward more labor-intensively produced wage goods to a drop in population growth rates as a result of greater personal fulfillment and family security.

The employment problem must be attacked in all sectors of the economy, although each presents its own particular obstacles. Agriculture already absorbs half of the region's work force, and it appears that difficult institutional changes, such as comprehensive land reform and the introduction of effective systems for the delivery of farm services, are required before more full-time job opportunities can be provided in significant numbers. At the same time, there has been a very slow rate of growth in employment in other sectors. Services absorb the largest portion of urban work forces, but underemployment is already rampant. Construction programs have a definite role to play, but the small size of this sector limits its potential impact. While artisan production offers employment possibilities, modern manufacturing is displacing a good deal of this activity. Accordingly, the factories of Latin America must increase their rate of job creation in light of their rapidly increasing production and the migration to the cities that this has generated. Thus far, they have not met this challenge: in the postwar period employment in the region's factories has grown only half as fast as manufacturing output.

Indirect employment effects of modern manufacturing are not substantial. Indications are that the employment multiplier is small for open economies utilizing capital-intensive production methods. In addition, this type of investment, assisted by easier access to cheap capital, tends to displace smaller, labor-intensive enterprises and their suppliers. There is no reason to believe that labor-intensive production would create any fewer jobs indirectly, particularly in view of the additional demand for wage goods this would stimulate and the local linkages it would create.

Direct manufacturing employment can be expanded in three basic ways. Production processes can be changed, the product mix can be altered, and markets, both domestic and foreign, can be enlarged. The three can be compatible. Labor-intensive production results in more equal income distribution, which in turn increases the size of the domestic market and fosters a demand for a different type of good. Although the export potential now appears greater for the products of the more modern industries, many of these (e.g., electronics, office machinery, motor vehicles, transport equipment) can also be produced more labor-intensively. At the same time, there are distinct advantages to using more labor in the production process. These include the provision of more jobs from the same amount of (scarce) capital, the abundance of relatively cheap labor, more equal income distribution, the creation rather than displacement of traditional jobs, and the appropriateness of labor-intensive technologies for small-scale operations and smaller-size markets.

Yet, the capital/labor ratio in Latin American industry continues to increase. It is argued in some circles that, while the introduction of more labor-intensive production can provide some additional jobs in the short run, in the longer term capital-intensive production generates greater employment through higher economic growth rates and consequent "trickle down" effects. This argument, however, has found no substantiation in the developments of the past three decades. Unprecedented rates of industrial growth founded in policies of technological modernization have been paralleled by declining rates of labor absorption.

Another unsubstantiated argument is that the main difficulty in adapting production processes to utilize more labor lies in real technological fixity. To the contrary, there exist possibilities for greater labor substitution in the already relatively labor-intensive, traditional industries (e.g., textiles, clothing, footwear, leather goods, furniture, rubber products, wood products), as well as in the more dynamic industries, such as those mentioned above. Continuous-process industries have rather limited scope for capital displacement in comparison with those that are product-centered. The former have a central mechanical or chemical process which is carried out in a series of machine-controlled operations and in which there are limited possibilities for factor substitution. These industries include chemicals, petrochemicals, metal refining, oil refining, and brewing. The latter, on the other hand, include the manufacturing and assembly of such products as automotive, mechanical, and electrical equipment and involve the integration of a multiplicity of distinct steps as opposed to basically indivisible central processes.

Rather than technological rigidity, the central question involved in a decision on labor-capital substitution is often one of plant efficiency or product quality. While it has been demonstrated in developing countries, such as Indonesia, that less capital-intensive production can yield high-quality goods at competitive costs, it has been found that Latin American industries that use sophisticated technology from the United States or Western Europe frequently do so less efficiently and with higher costs than do their counterparts in these developed nations.

There are many other ways in which greater use can be made of labor in manufacturing. Ancillary operations—materials handling, packing, grading, finishing, in-factory transportation, storage, distribution, etc.—constitute a substantial part of production processes, and all these movements toward and away from a central mechanical process can be performed manually. Smaller-scale operations are usually more labor-intensive, since ancillary operations constitute a greater proportion of total factory activity; in addition, many traditional industries do not suffer from diseconomies of scale if they are designed to take advantage of low labor costs. Finally, multiple work shifts could provide additional employment opportunities if institutional and legal barriers—particularly statutes dealing with overtime and female employment—were to be removed.

An examination of various industries reveals that there are few in which the potential for increased labor substitution does not exist. It has been found in the manufacture of such diverse products as textiles, chemicals, cement, and paint, as well as in the processing of some foods, that employment can be increased in relative terms by scaling down production. In addition to producing for smaller markets, more labor-absorbing methods can be utilized to process foods for poorer and less-demanding consumers without adversely affecting the nutritional and health aspects of product quality. In some industries, including plastic products, shoes, and can manufacturing, the central mechanical transforming process allows for the use of automatic, intermediate, or labor-intensive techniques without sacrificing the quality of the finished good. In any event, ancillary activities are greater labor-absorbers than are central manufacturing processes and can be major sources of employment in a wide range of industries, including paint production, corn and fruit processing, food canning, soft-drink bottling, woodmaking, and electronics.

If industrial technology contains this degree of flexibility, the explanation for the general preference in Latin America for capital-intensive technologies must be found elsewhere. Distorted factor prices, emphasis upon labor productivity, and other economic factors contribute significantly to these preferences. As labor is not the scarcest resource in the region, it is not logical to concentrate on maximizing its productivity rather than that of capital. An emphasis on increasing output by upgrading workers' skills rather than by increasing the size of the work force raises the wages of a relative few while fostering a stagnation in the growth of employment. If the productivity of labor is to become a measure of true economic development for *all* members of society, it should be taken as an average for the entire population.

In light of the continent's abundance of labor, wage levels are high. In good part, this is caused by the widespread practice on the part of the past generation of Latin American leaders of engendering support of urban workers and labor unions for political gain. Many unions have been able to convert their power into concrete advantages for their members while demonstrating little concern about the unemployed. Fringe benefits in some countries can constitute close to half of a worker's cost to a company and are as much a cause of mechanization as are minimum wage statutes. In addition, many countries have legislated barriers to the dismissal of employees which, while protecting the latter, further encourage the investor to mechanize his operations. A rational policy would be to allow wages in the modern industrial sector to rise,.but not too abruptly. They should be linked, as has been the case in Brazil, more closely to changes in the cost of living than to increases in productivity.

The introduction of labor-intensive technologies may run up against a more formidable labor-related obstacle—a shortage of the necessary skilled personnel. While increased supervision can compensate for workers' inexpertness in particular processes or for deficiencies in coordinating activities, the problem is that good supervisory personnel is also difficult to find. In fact, this particular shortage is often cited by managers as a principal reason for a high degree of mechanization. In some industries, however, the importance of capable supervisors is diminished by the high degree of latitude permissible in product quality. In others, a machine-paced operation can be used, maintaining a relatively low level of mechanization and permitting the use of unskilled in place of skilled labor.

While labor is often overpriced, capital in Latin America is usually underpriced. In fact, interest rates in some countries are often well below the rate of inflation. This creates a great demand for funds, with the lion's share being cornered by the larger, more mechanized concerns. Higher interest rates would increase the labor-intensivity of these large firms and make more capital available to small enterprises, while encouraging greater saving and thus capital formation. The importation of machinery and equipment is made cheaper by overvalued and preferential exchange rates and by tariff exemptions. If this situation were rectified, and changes were also made in tax, depreciation allowance, and interest rate policies, many companies would be forced to use more labor in their operations.

Multinational corporations, as a rule, are not as influenced in their choice of technology by factor prices as are domestic companies. The former can raise funds in international markets and can often borrow at preferential rates in Latin America. Nor are wage levels a determining factor. The principal determinants in the foreign firm's selection of production techniques appear to be factor prices in the home country, exchange rates, import duties, methods of depreciation, market size, fringe benefits, the character of the work force, and strict laws regarding the dismissal of employees. Most MNCs deal with these problems by engineering their way around them.

Latin American companies often take the same approach, utilizing capital-intensive methods developed in the industrialized countries. Little effort has been made to create indigenous R, D & E capabilities that would be able to develop more appropriate technologies. Too much emphasis is placed upon basic research rather than on finding solutions to practical industrial problems. Part of the problem lies in the emigration and hence shortage of talented engineers, but those who remain and the businessmen they consult often possess biases in favor of "sophisticated" techniques. Cultural factors may be partially accountable for these preferences, as is the educational system, particularly schools of engineering and economics, both in Latin America and the United States. There is a great need to train future decision-makers, in both the public and private sectors, in a manner that is relevant to the circumstances that exist in their respective countries.

Basically, there are three ways to attain appropriate technologies. The simplest is to import second-hand machinery from the developed countries or to use old blueprints to produce such equipment. The disadvantages of this approach include the rather common belief among Latin Americans that this represents an attempt by the industrialized countries to foist "second-class development" on them; the possibility that capital, as well as labor, costs will be greater because of the machines' absolute obsolescence; high dismantling, shipping, maintenance, and repair costs; and the possible unavailability of spare parts. On the other hand, second-hand machinery is frequently quite inexpensive, efficient, and labor-intensive. Furthermore, the greater maintenance requirements provide many more employment opportunities.

Another and most promising route to labor-intensive technologies is the adaptation of techniques developed in the industrialized nations to meet the labor-absorbing needs of Latin America. This was the basic approach employed by Japan during its industrial development. Unfortunately, however, Latin America lacks the technological base that existed in Japan during its early stage of industrialization. It would, nevertheless, be advantageous to tackle such an undertaking and to "learn by doing," but most of the region's engineers have not shown themselves prepared to risk innovative activity.

A third approach is the creation of new technologies. In light of the high costs this entails, the duplication of activity in the developed countries it would surely involve, and the shortage of resources in Latin America, this method should be used selectively. In general, a choice among the three routes to labor-intensive technologies should be determined on a case-by-case basis.

It is essential that these creative and adaptive activities be undertaken in Latin America. Overdependence upon R, D & E centers in the developed countries can be counterproductive, as their scientists and engineers frequently lack experience in the region and knowledge of conditions there and suffer the additional disadvantage of being far away from their clients. Location within Latin America is preferable for the ease with which direct communications with clients can be established and the ability to test findings immediately under local conditions. Unfortunately, such facilities are not common in Latin America. Considering their cost, it would be preferable to set up regional centers, but progress in this direction has been blocked by a lack of intercountry cooperation.

There are several institutions within which such work could be done. Universities would not be one of the best places, although they do possess the necessary facilities. Generally, the academic community is neither oriented to, nor interested in, dealing with practical industrial problems. Furthermore, the possibility of disruptions in university activities and in government-university relations make both the continuity and the funding of such work rather tenuous propositions.

A public agency may also be an inappropriate location for R, D & E because of the potential for government interference for political reasons. Government agencies also suffer from their limited contact with industry. On the other hand, government involvement is often warranted by the absence of a viable patent system, economies of scale, and the necessity to assure that the R, D & E undertaken fit the country's development requirements.

Independent agencies, publicly or privately financed, can usually only fill the gaps left by other institutions. Private companies, on the other hand, can be ideal places for industrial R, D & E because of their orientation to practical problem-solving and the rapidity with which their developments can be introduced. Many firms, however, have neither the technical expertise nor the resources to undertake this type of activity, while others find no incentives within a protected market for doing so.

The subsidiaries of multinational corporations are perhaps best suited of all institutions within Latin America for developing technologies appropriate to the region's conditions and factor endowments. They possess both the scale of operation and the technical expertise to justify the cost of independent research. The impact of this innovation would be considerable because of linkages back to the subsidiary's domestic suppliers, to whom managerial and technical assistance could be rendered. MNCs could also coordinate and upgrade the capabilities of other local R, D & E institutions.

Thus far, however, the MNC has done little in the way of developing labor-intensive technologies. Several factors account for this: protected markets, shortage of skilled personnel in Latin America, difficulty in inducing highly qualified Americans to leave the United States, desire to maintain high product standards, failure of the MNC to fully perceive the problem, local government desire for "modern" technology, poor patent systems, and unstable political and economic conditions.

There is little reason to believe that, given these factors and the

MNC's far greater familiarity with capital-intensive techniques, the typical MNC will undertake the development of more appropriate technologies on its own. Large international firms are usually especially protective of their patents and trademarks and will refuse to downgrade the latter, especially if they are producing for export. Furthermore, most foreign corporations simply to not consider it in their interest to transfer design and engineering capabilities to firms with which they have, at best, only a technical connection.

Yet it is imperative that Latin American governments pressure the MNC into adopting appropriate technologies, because of the corporation's influence and impact on local economies. Its demonstration effect lies not only in the technology it uses but also in the wages it pays, as it can raise the pay scale of an entire industry. To the extent that this were to happen, it would discourage the use of labor vis-à-vis capital. MNCs can also dominate the credit supply from local money markets, thereby depriving more labor-intensive, indigenous firms of their basic capital requirements.

MNCs can also displace domestic enterprises by introducing products that do not require indigenous materials or components for their manufacture. In general, foreign firms tend to use Latin American suppliers less frequently than do their local counterparts. It is true that problems of cost, quality, and delivery are involved, but these can be overcome in time, particularly with managerial and technical assistance. These linkages are worth encouraging because of the large amounts of employment that can consequently be generated.

MNCs, themselves, could also operate in a more labor-intensive fashion, even in the export sector, as their technical capabilities should in most cases be able to guarantee product quality. They are also in a position to help create new industrial systems that would increase the technological independence of Latin American countries. Yet, as discussed earlier, few large corporations see it as being to their advantage to share their knowledge and capabilities with governments or competing enterprises.

Such positive action on the part of the MNC, however, is as much in its own interest as in that of Latin America itself. American business leaders emphasize the importance of a stable investment environment, yet that very stability is being undermined by the discontent and unrest that the employment crisis is provoking. Because of the impact that foreign firms have on most of the region's economies, they themselves could make a significant contribution to the problem's resolution. Where participation in this effort would place some firms at a short-term competitive disadvantage, governments should establish regulations that would require all companies to undertake certain employment-promoting activities.

There are many, however, including businessmen, who feel that

[133]

MNCs do not possess the flexibility to alter their production techniques and employ more Latin Americans directly. They are seen, in this view, to be too large and entrenched in their ways and too accustomed to the use of high-volume production methods to make any significant changes. Furthermore, many MNC managers look down on the utilization of unsophisticated machinery, know little about the culture in which they are operating, and do not agree that it is their responsibility to generate employment directly. Rather, they emphasize the need to maximize growth—a task in which they feel they can play a central role.

When this philosophy and inflexibility are combined with a protected market, cheap capital, abundant fringe benefits, and various other labor-related difficulties, there is little hope that the MNC will seek, on its own initiative, to alter its production techniques to utilize more labor. In order to tap the resources in the possession of the MNC, national governments or regional blocs will therefore have to provide incentives and impose requirements selectively.

It is fair to say, as a general statement, however, that Latin American governments have not given employment generation a high priority in their respective economic plans. Their general biases toward the use of capital-intensive technology instead of job-creating production methods in the manufacturing sector were reflected at the CACTAL meetings in Brasilia in 1972. It is not surprising, therefore, that these governments currently do not appear ready to pressure MNCs on the employment issue, despite their increased bargaining power. Rather, the growing emphasis has been upon MNC capital-intensive export promotion.

Although the Brazilian government claims to be zeroing in on the country's employment problem, it has been stressing capital-intensive production and has opened the doors to foreign investment without regard to the job-creating potential of the technology imported. Mexico likewise has rejected the labor-intensive approach and has been unsuccessful in creating the jobs required for its rapidly growing work force. The Andean Pact does limit the entry of foreign capital but makes little or no mention of the implications this investment may have for new employment opportunities within its member countries. These countries individually, however, are now showing some sensitivity to the problems of the un- and underemployed. Until recently, Colombia had all but ignored the recommendations of the ILO employment team, but the government is now attempting to expand job opportunities through, among other means, efficient credit facilities for small- and medium-sized industry. Venezuela has lately taken a number of steps aimed at creating new jobs in the service sector but, despite having shown some interest in alternative technologies, continues to favor capital-intensive industrial investment. Furthermore, throughout

Latin America, factor prices remain considerably distorted, contributing to the underutilization of labor in its production processes.

Governments could help rectify this situation by using their influence over MNCs, in particular, and their respective economies, in general. Relative factor prices can be altered, for instance. Policies regarding the cost of labor should go beyond wage restraint in the modern sector (a subsidization of low-paid labor might also be effective) and incorporate such proposals as the elimination of payroll taxes, the cutting of the link between the financing of social security schemes and a company's wage bill, the allowance of write-offs for training expenses, and the modification of labor laws relating to women, overtime, and the dismissal of employees (since restrictive firing laws influence original investment decisions toward greater capital-intensivity). The raising of interest rates, the downward realignment of exchange rates, a deceleration of depreciation rates, the elimination of tax incentives that lead to capital-intensive reinvestment, and the raising of tariffs on heavy machinery should all be given consideration when attempting to increase the real price of capital. In addition, less protection should be given to import-substitution industries, and a variety of means, including tax concessions, revised patent laws, and contract stipulations, can be employed to induce a greater contribution by MNCs to local R, D & E efforts. The creation of the right economic environment must accompany any contractual demands on MNCs to employ a specific number of workers or utilize a more labor-intensive technology.

Most MNC executives, however, do not believe that Latin American governments will make such demands upon them, but in the event that they do, the former say that they are prepared to leave. Similar threats in the past, though, have not been carried out, as foreign corporations have usually found ways to adapt to new circumstances. Even when pressured, the MNC usually remains in Latin America for the same reasons it originally invested there—access to vital resources and particular markets, location for exporting, and tax advantages, among others. In addition, once a manufacturing affiliate is established, the difficulties and expense involved in moving it are generally greater than the extra inconveniences that might be imposed upon it.

The bargaining strength of Latin American governments, however, is subject to serious limitations, particularly when they are seeking to attract new investment. The MNC's superior skill in the negotiating process and its greater knowledge of investment alternatives give it a distinct advantage in maintaining exclusive control of its technological capabilities. Hence, the region's governments might choose instead to expand their relationships with small- and medium-sized firms, which are generally more adaptive in their technology and more flexible about sharing it.

The trend, however, in the gradually shifting balance of power between even the larger foreign corporations and the region's governments has been favoring the latter, as these countries become more cognizant of relative bargaining strengths. Their ability to play off one international investor against another increases the more that Japanese and European companies offer alternatives to U.S. investment. The Japanese, in fact, may become pace-setters in the changing role of foreign enterprise, as they have developed a high degree of flexibility in many areas, including an ability to use relatively large amounts of unskilled labor efficiently in their operations. Hence, in some cases, Latin American governments may already be in a position to enlist the support of the MNC in an integrated and comprehensive attack on their unemployment problems.

At the core of such an undertaking must be a policy of industrial decentralization, which takes employment opportunities to the people. Not only would a network of regional growth centers and agroindustrial and marketing towns slow the rate of migration to the large urban areas, but the nature of the production facilities thus established would be proportionally more labor-intensive. Producing for smaller and lower-income markets, these enterprises tend to be smaller themselves, employ technologies that make greater use of local resources (including labor) and the products of local suppliers, and produce goods more appropriate to the needs of the region's poor.

The pattern of income distribution is largely responsible for the type of product mix, which in turn strongly influences the general character of the technology employed. Governments could directly promote the use of labor-absorbing technology by assuring a market for products manufactured in this fashion, but the most effective way of fostering this type of production is to increase the purchasing power of the poor. In light of the political realities of Latin America, this can best be accomplished by combining production and income distribution in one process. This requires the provision of more jobs in each rurally based enterprise and in its complementary industries.

MNCs cannot be expected to locate in nonindustrialized areas, however, without the necessary infrastructure being provided by governments. If construction of transportation, communications, housing, power, and water systems is undertaken through a rural works program implemented and controlled at the local level, a vast number of jobs, both full- and part-time, can be created. On the other hand, increased sophistication in the negotiating process has enabled some governments to shift this financial burden to the investing company in many instances. Companies are often willing to absorb this cost in countries with political and economic stability, especially where the value of the property they have purchased will be enhanced.

Foreign firms have made significant contributions in Latin America in such areas as the production of essential investment goods, the earning of foreign exchange through exportation, and the introduction of managerial, technical, and marketing skills. At the same time, however, their presence has been counterproductive in the region's development to the extent that they have not fully utilized available local resources and have not produced to meet the needs of the vast majority of Latin Americans. The use of capital-intensive technology limits the number of people that can be absorbed into the production process, while stimulating additional migration to the cities through the higher wages it generates. Capital-intensive production in these open economies also utilizes considerable amounts of foreign inputs instead of local goods and suppliers.

Nevertheless, the MNC can still make a contribution to a broadly-based development effort. It possesses the resources required to develop more appropriate technologies, it has the power through direct assistance or demonstration effect to persuade local enterprises and local institutions to do the same, it can stimulate local small-scale industry by increasing its purchases from indigenous suppliers, and it can change its product mix or alter its product design to better accommodate the needs of the poor. Latin American governments have the responsibility to offer the right incentives, impose the necessary requirements, and create the proper economic environment to induce foreign companies to adopt this new role.

Given the inclination of most engineers to design highly mechanized plants without regard to local economic factors, governments have the additional responsibility to reorient this engineering approach. They need to concentrate on the training of development engineers and encourage a greater integration and understanding among engineers, economists, and businessmen. At the same time, however, distorted factor prices should be realigned, for they can only reinforce this engineering bias.

Unfortunately, the region's governments do not perceive the employment crisis to be as critical as it is. As a result, no comprehensive approach has been taken to the problem and little or no pressure has been exerted upon foreign firms to make a contribution in this area. MNCs generally do not believe that employment generation will be among the growing number of demands made upon them by Latin American countries in the near future. Concerned by other nationalistic and leftist pressures, these investors appear to perceive the employment issue as rather peripheral to their operations and to their future in Latin America. But governments and firms alike, by their current inaction, are only hastening the arrival of the day when internal political pressures will force an alternative approach to employment problems.

The explosive potential of the circumstances that exist in much of Latin America today stems in good part from a growing awareness by many of the expanding economic opportunities and benefits accruing to the relative few. As Raúl Prebisch points out, mass communication has brought the "beguiling mirage of city life" to the rural population. But this life soon becomes a "hotbed of tormenting frustration: the frustration bred of social marginality." The "rural and urban masses are awakening to consciousness of their long-forgotten dignity as human beings."[1]

Modern industrial expansion in Latin America has effected some basic social and economic change in the region, while by its very nature simultaneously sowing the seeds for popular frustration and unrest. Ulla Olin of the United Nations Development Program argues that

... revolutionary movements are most likely to occur in the wake of major social and economic transformations, which have upset the pre-existing social organization. New opportunities have been created, which attract a substantial following. Many of those who actively seek to join the bandwagon will succeed, many will fail. Additionally, the introduction of new methods of production and management will render previous methods obsolete and their adherents surplus. Success and failure will occur in all gradations, with the final outcome often unpredictable at one particular moment. .... Because of the tendency of both success and failure to be to an extent self-sustaining, it is inherent in such a situation that the gap between social groups will tend to widen. This will intensify the pain of failure, regardless of whether the actual level of living is declining or not.[2]

Olin goes on to select employment creation—particularly for the potential rural migrants—as the most basic and urgent need in these countries and feels that if left unattended, "the situation will eventually seek its own, probably far costlier, solution."[3]

Will it take a crisis situation to force Latin American governments to act decisively to resolve this problem? That does appear to be the case. Un- and underemployment in the region are already of critical proportions, but little more than words have been forthcoming in response. Pressure from below will continue to increase, however, and spokesmen for the cause will continue to arise from the church, the military, and other groups. The ability of individual governments to cope with these internal pressures for more social justice will determine their respective political fates. Rational leadership, which turns away from the growth-means-development philosophy and takes aggressive, comprehensive action upon confronting the realities of the job crisis, should not only survive but also broaden its political base. Governments that continue to ignore the warning signals will be in increasing danger of being toppled.

Political stability is in the interest not only of political rulers but also of other vested interests, including the foreign corporation. It is thus in their collective interest to tackle the employment problem—immediately and aggressively. For, as the OECD has recently stated, "without major new initiatives, not now even on the horizon, the burden of unemployment by 1980 will have created explosive, if not exploded, social and political crises in nearly all developing countries."[4] Unless there is a rapid awakening to the magnitude of the unemployment problem, accompanied by the necessary policies and action, Latin America, by all present indications, is entering just such a critical period.

NOTES

CHAPTER 1

1. MacEoin, *Revolution*, p. 22.
2. See Prebisch, *Change*, pp. 20, 109; and Jones, "Underutilization," pp. 451-469.
3. International Labour Office (ILO), *Full*, pp. 42-43.
4. Grant, "Accelerating," p. 3.
5. See OECD study in Thorbecke, "Unemployment," p. 7.
6. See Nelson, Schultz, and Slighton, *Structural*, pp. 151-152.
7. Organization of American States (OAS), "Document," p. 77; and Bradford, *Forces*, p. 2.
8. Kendall, in O'Shaughnessy, et al, "Financial," p. 26.
9. See OAS study in Thorbecke, "Unemployment," p. 10.
10. U.S. Bureau of Labor Statistics, "Labor," pp. 34-36.
11. ILO, *Full*.
12. Bradford, *Forces*, p. 29.
13. Economist Intelligence Unit, *QER: Colombia-Ecuador*, Annual Supplement, 1972, p. 2.
14. ILO, *Full*, pp. 362-363.
15. Ibid., pp. 13, 45-46.
16. Haq, "Employment," p. 3.
17. Business International, *Venezuela*, p. 17.
18. Economist Intelligence Unit, *QER: Brazil*, No. 1, 1973, pp. 4-5.
19. Grant, "Equal," p. 2.
20. Grant, "Accelerating," p. 3.
21. Reynolds and Gregory, *Wages*, pp. 35, 303.
22. ILO, *Full*, p. 21.
23. See Chandavarkar, "Growth," p. 31.
24. See Jackson, "Technologies," p. 13.
25. Prebisch, *Change*, p. 37.
26. Rich, *Families*, p. 24.
27. Abbott, "Women," pp. 24-25.
28. For an interesting discussion of discrimination against female workers in Latin America, see Keremitsis, "Workers."
29. See ILO, *Full*, Appendix A.
30. Ibid., p. 14.

NOTES

31. Hall, "Attitudes," p. 53.

CHAPTER 2
1. Prebisch, *Change*, pp. 28-30.
2. Seers, *Full*, p. 34.
3. See Ramos, *Labor*, p. 160, for argument presented by K. Arrow, H. Chenery, B. Minhas, and R. Solow in "Capital-Labor Substitution and Economic Efficiency," *Review of Economics and Statistics*, August 1961.
4. Prebisch, *Change*, p. 4.
5. Baer and Hervé, "Employment," p. 89.
6. Prebisch, *Change*, p. 73.
7. Owens and Shaw, *Development*, p. 108.
8. Prebisch, *Change*, pp. 28, 33.
9. Bradford, *Forces*, p. 21.
10. Thorbecke, "Unemployment," p. 9.
11. See Economist Intelligence Unit, *QER: Brazil*, Annual Supplement, 1972, p. 3; and *QER: Colombia-Ecuador*, Annual Supplement, 1972, p. 2.
12. Jackson, "Technologies," p. 21.
13. ILO, *Full*, pp. 127-128.
14. Bradford, *Forces*, pp. 38-39.
15. Zschock, *Manpower*, p. 51.
16. Ibid.
17. Prebisch, *Change*, p. 43.
18. See Slawinski, "Prospects," p. 182.
19. See Bradford, *Forces*, p. 22.
20. Zschock, *Manpower*, p. 135.
21. Baer and Hervé, "Employment," pp. 89-90.
22. See Poats, *Technology*, pp. 55-56.
23. Nelson, Schultz, and Slighton, *Structural*, p. 127; and Economist Intelligence Unit, *QER: Colombia-Ecuador*, Annual Supplement, 1972, p. 2.
24. ILO, *Full*, pp. 34, 113.
25. Ibid., p. 107.
26. Nelson, Schultz, and Slighton, *Structural*, p. 127.
27. Junta de Planificación, *Informe*,

pp. 38, 73, 85.
28. See Bradford, *Forces*, p. 37.
29. Ibid., p. 38.
30. UNIDO, *Small-Scale*, p. 51.
31. Baranson, *Industrial*, p. 9; and Baranson, "Employment," p. 26.
32. See Galenson, "Development," pp. 506-518.
33. See Baranson, *Industrial*, p. 15.
34. Baer and Hervé, "Employment," p. 107.
35. See Bradford, *Forces*, p. 27.
36. Marsden, "Progressive," p. 480.
37. Jackson, "Technologies," p. 15.
38. Chandavarkar, "Growth," p. 32.
39. Ramos, *Labor*, p. 157.
40. Chudson, *International*, p. 48.
41. Bradford, *Forces*, pp. 37, 49.
42. Mason, *Transfer*, pp. 24-33.
43. See Hoda, "Development," p. 280.
44. Clarke, "Need," p. 260.
45. Clarke, *Experiment*, p. 19.
46. Slawinski, "Prospects," pp. 182-183.
47. Prebisch, *Change*, p. 213.
48. ILO, *Full*, p. 113.
49. Sabolo, "Sectoral," p. 467.
50. ILO, *Full*, p. 113.
51. See Baranson, "Employment," p. 22; and Baranson, *Industrial*, pp. 15-16.
52. Hirshman, *Strategy*, pp. 147-148.
53. Stanford Research Institute, *Manual*, p. 148.
54. See Marsden, "Progressive," p. 489.
55. Hirshman, *Strategy*, p. 131.
56. Hagen, *Economics*, p. 98.
57. Baranson, *Industrial*, p. 13.
58. Clarke, *Experiment*, p. 18.

CHAPTER 3
1. Mason, *Transfer*, p. 61.
2. Jackson, "Technologies," p. 21.
3. Hagen, *Economics*, pp. 424-425.
4. Stanford, *Manual*, pp. 100-101.
5. ILO, *Full*, p. 169.
6. Chudson, *International*, p. 16.
7. Grant, "Multinational," p. 11.

8. See Bradford, *Forces*, pp. 24-25.
9. ILO, *Full*, pp. 110-111.
10. Chudson, *International*, p. 32.
11. Baranson, *Industrial*, p. 101.
12. van Houten, "Assembly," pp. 21-22.
13. Ranis, "Industrial," p. 407.
14. Baranson, "Employment," p. 24.
15. Baranson, *Industrial*, p. 13.
16. Jackson, "Technologies," p. 20.
17. Hirshman, *Strategy*, p. 151.
18. Hagen, *Economics*, pp. 424-425.
19. Hirshman, *Strategy*, pp. 147-152.
20. Ibid., pp. 145-146.
21. Clague, "Determinants," pp. 188-205.
22. Reynolds and Gregory, *Wages*, p. 188.
23. Baranson, *Industrial*, pp. 17, 83.
24. Wells, "Man," pp. 11-12.
25. United Nations, *Panel*, p. 20.
26. Ibid., p. 22.
27. Vernon, *Sovereignty*, pp. 183-184.
28. Wells, "Man," p. 12.
29. Hirshman, *Strategy*, p. 151.
30. Mason, *Transfer*, p. 58.
31. Strassmann, *Change*, pp. 163-164.
32. Morgan, "Transfer," p. 147.
33. Ozawa, *Transfer*, p. 25.
34. See UNIDO, *Small-Scale*, p. 51.
35. Chudson, *International*, p. 32.
36. UNIDO, *Small-Scale*, p. 65.
37. UN, *Panel*, pp. 21-22.
38. Mason, *Transfer*, p. 54; see also Baranson, *Industrial*, pp. 12-13.
39. Chudson, *International*, p. 26.
40. Baranson, "Multinational," p. 2.
41. Ranis, "Industrial," pp. 407-408.
42. See de la Torre, "Investment," for citation of the product life cycle approach of Louis T. Wells, Jr.
43. Baranson, *Industrial*, p. 12.
44. ILO, *Full*, p. 117.
45. Strassmann, *Change*, pp. 178-179.
46. ILO, *Full*, pp. 202-203.
47. PREALC, *Situación*, pp. 143-144.
48. ILO, *Full*, pp. 206-207.
49. UNIDO, *Textile*, p. 39.
50. Ibid., pp. 43-47.
51. Grant, "Multinational," p. 13.
52. UNIDO, *Textile*, p. 55.
53. Keremitsis, "Women," pp. 4-11.
54. Ranis, "Industrial," p. 399; see also Baranson, *Industrial*, p. 9.
55. See UNIDO, *Textile*, pp. 43-44.
56. Baer and Hervé, "Employment," p. 90.
57. See Stanford, *Manual*, p. 99.
58. See Baer and Hervé, "Employment," p. 95.
59. UNIDO, *Textile*, pp. 31-32, 57.
60. UNIDO, *Chemical*, pp. 42-43.
61. Giral and Morgan, *Chemical*, pp. 2, 102-103.
62. Ibid., pp. 9-10.
63. See Chudson, *International*, p. 33.
64. UNIDO, *Chemical*, p. 43.
65. Ibid.
66. Giral and Morgan, *Chemical*, p. 129.
67. Strassmann, *Change*, pp. 163-164.
68. Baranson, "Employment," p. 26; see also Chudson, *International*, p. 31.
69. Pickett, "Choice," pp. 219-220.
70. Ibid., p. 213.
71. Pack, "Use," pp. 46-47.
72. Ibid., pp. 47-48.
73. Wells, "Man," p. A-2.
74. Baranson, "Employment," p. 23.
75. Stanford, *Manual*, pp. 76-79; and Wells, "Man," p. A-3.
76. Grant, "Equal," p. 10.
77. Stanford, *Manual*, pp. 35-39.
78. See Wells, "Man," p. A-4.
79. Pickett, "Choice," pp. 8-10.
80. Marsden, "Progressive," p. 497.
81. See Stanford, *Manual*, pp. 27-30; and ILO, *Employment*, pp. 371-376.
82. Juma and Routh, "Production," pp. 195-209.
83. Stanford, *Manual*, pp. 12-16.
84. Ibid., pp. 64-66.
85. See Wells, "Man," p. A-3.
86. UNIDO, *Estimation*, pp. 41-43.

87. Sigurdson, "Technology," p. 9.
88. UNIDO, *Estimation*, p. 41.
89. See Chudson, *International*, p. 16; and Stanford, *Manual*, pp. 52-54.
90. Ranis, "Industrial," p. 403.
91. Ibid.
92. Ibid., pp. 406-407.
93. Grant, "Equal," pp. 8-9.

CHAPTER 4
1. Seers, *Full*, p. 109.
2. See Bradford, *Forces*, p. 29.
3. Thorbecke, "Unemployment," p. 19.
4. See Jackson, "Technologies," p. 17.
5. Alexander, *Labor*, p. 17.
6. Alba, *Politics*, p. 346.
7. See Goodman, "Distribution," pp. 137-140.
8. ILO, *Full*, pp. 187-188.
9. Reynolds and Gregory, *Wages*, p. 88.
10. Mason, *Transfer*, p. 11.
11. ILO, *Full*, pp. 200-202.
12. Reynolds and Gregory, *Wages*, p. 156.
13. Baranson, *Manufacturing*, p. 14.
14. Strassmann, *Change*, p. 93.
15. Business International, *Brazil*, p. 15.
16. See Economist Intelligence Unit, *QER: Brazil*, Annual Supplement, 1972, p. 11; and *QER: Brazil*, No. 1, 1973, p. 18.
17. See Ranis, "Industrial," pp. 402-406.
18. Weed, "Considerations," p. 8.
19. See Nelson, Schultz, and Slighton, *Structural*, pp. 199-203.
20. Mason, *Transfer*, p. 12.
21. Baranson, "Efforts," p. 11.
22. See Vernon, *Sovereignty*, p. 99.

CHAPTER 5
1. Higgins, *Development*, p. 258.
2. Baer and Hervé, "Employment," p. 93.
3. Urquidi, "Implications," p. 102.
4. See Baranson, "Efforts," p. 3; and Baranson, "Role," p. 17.

5. Nelson, Schultz, and Slighton, *Structural*, p. 288.
6. Hagen, *Economics*, p. 431.
7. National Academy of Sciences, *R, D & E*, p. 42.
8. Strassmann, *Change*, pp. 35-42.
9. Pickett, "Choice," pp. 216-217.
10. Ibid., p. 217.
11. Strassmann, *Change*, pp. 141-144.
12. See Baranson, *Industrial*, pp. 4-5; and Baranson, "Role," p. 18.
13. Macrae, "Future," pp. xxix-xxx.
14. For a more comprehensive view of these aspects of Japanese industrial development, see Ranis, "Industrial," p. 397; Baranson, "Employment," p. 25; Baranson, "Industrial," p. 17; Morgan, "Transfer," pp. 145-146; and Giral and Morgan, *Chemical*, pp. 136-137.
15. Giral and Morgan, *Chemical*, p. 101.
16. Strassmann, *Change*, p. 270.
17. Clarke, *Experiment*, pp. 18, 43.
18. Weed, "Considerations," pp. 9-10.
19. Clarke, *Experiment*, p. 46.
20. Strassmann, *Change*, p. 48.
21. Giral and Morgan, *Chemical*, pp. 138-139.
22. Clarke, *Experiment*, p. 22.
23. Weed, "Considerations," p. 14.
24. UNIDO, *Research*, pp. 9-11, 26.
25. See Andean Common Market, *Agreement*, Article 40, p. 12; and "Decision No. 24," Article 23, p. 9.
26. See UNIDO, *Research*, p. 28.
27. Ibid., pp. 29-32.
28. Strassmann, *Change*, p. 47.
29. Nelson, Schultz, and Slighton, *Structural*, pp. 289-291.
30. UNIDO, *Research*, p. 33.
31. Baranson, "Efforts," pp. 9-10.
32. UNIDO, *Research*, pp. 30-31.
33. See Baranson, "Efforts," p. 2.
34. See National Academy of Sciences, *R, D & E*, p. 13.
35. Baranson, *Manufacturing*, p. 122.
36. National Academy of Sciences, *R, D & E*, pp. 44-46.

37. Ibid.
38. Mason, *Transfer*, p. 54.
39. UN, *Panel*, p. 22.
40. Turner, *Multinational*, pp. 163-165.
41. Baranson, *Industrial*, p. 19.
42. Turner, *Multinational*, p. 201.
43. Baranson, *Manufacturing*, p. 124.
44. Business International, *Brazil*, p. 68.
45. Baranson, "Multinational," Abstract.
46. National Academy of Sciences, *R, D & E*, p. 11.

CHAPTER 6
1. Wells, "Man," pp. 3-5.
2. Chudson, *International*, pp. 27-28.
3. Strassmann, *Change*, pp. 141-147.
4. See Chudson, *International*, p. 28.
5. See Bradford, *Forces*, p. 12.
6. Business International, *Effects*, p. 93.
7. Mason, *Transfer*, pp. 19-20.
8. Blake, "Labor," p. 182.
9. See McMillan and González, with Erickson, *Enterprise*, p. 174.
10. Business International, *Brazil*, pp. 42-43.
11. Kreinin, "Effectiveness," pp. 136-137.
12. Hagen, *Economics*, p. 422.
13. Council of the Americas, "Effects" Section I, p. 2.
14. Friedlin and Lupo, "Investment," pp. 16-21; and Chung, "Property," pp. 24-34.
15. Vernon, *Sovereignty*, p. 22.
16. Council of the Americas, "Effects," Section III, p. 1.
17. Ibid., Section I, p. 3; II, 5; III, 5.
18. Chudson, *International*, p. 42.
19. Mason, *Transfer*, pp. 39-43, 62-63.
20. Ibid., p. 65.
21. Turner, *Multinational*, pp. 191-192.
22. Urquidi, "Implications," p. 113.
23. Andean Common Market, "Decision No. 24," p. 15.
24. Lauterbach, *Enterprise*, p. 118.
25. Rosenstein-Rodan, "Problems."

26. Utley, "Business," p. 84.
27. Ibid.; and Business International, *Nationalism*, p. 12.
28. Vernon, *Sovereignty*, p. 100.
29. Council of the Americas, "Effects," Section II, p. 7, and III, 7.
30. Business International, *Base*, p. 16.
31. Ranis, "Industrial," p. 404.
32. Utley, "Business," p. 80; Fritsch, *Progress*, pp. 4, 43-44; and Wood and Keyser, *Sears, Roebuck*, p. 47.
33. Mason, *Transfer*, p. 40.
34. See National Academy of Sciences, *R, D & E*.
35. Dennison, "Development."
36. Ibid., p. 6.
37. Ibid.
38. Baranson, "Role," pp. 18-19.
39. Clague, "Determinants," pp. 188-205.
40. Business International, *Nationalism*, p. 85.
41. Mason, *Transfer*, p. 59.
42. Margolies, "Multinational," p. 47.
43. Urquidi, "Implications," p. 113.
44. Grant, "Multinational," p. 2.
45. See National Academy of Sciences, *R, D & E*.
46. Baranson, *Manufacturing*, pp. 123-124; and *Industrial*, p. 52.
47. Mason, *Transfer*, p. 55.
48. Strassmann, *Change*, pp. 39-40.
49. Mason, *Transfer*, p. 56.
50. Baranson, *Transfer*.
51. Johnson, "Multinational," p. 26.
52. UN, *Panel*, pp. 10-11.
53. Dennison, "Role," p. 15.
54. Council of the Americas, *Report*.

CHAPTER 7
1. Vernon, *Sovereignty*, p. 185.
2. ILO, *Full*, p. 161.
3. OAS, *Science*, p. 7.
4. OAS, "Document," p. 81.
5. Gabriel, "Capabilities"; and Baranson, "Multinational," pp. 6-7.
6. Grant, "Multinational," pp. 22-23.

NOTES

7. Bradford, *Forces*, p. 36.
8. Ibid., p. 44.
9. Baranson, "Role," p. 18.
10. Federative Republic of Brazil, *Plan*, pp. 16, 55.
11. See Economist Intelligence Unit, *QER: Brazil*, No. 1, 1973, p. 10.
12. Business International, *Brazil*, p. 9.
13. Economist Intelligence Unit, *QER: Brazil*, No. 1, 1973, p. 15.
14. Business International, *Brazil*, p. 8.
15. Brazil, *Plan*, p. 31.
16. Business International, *Brazil*, p. 8.
17. Brazil, *Plan*, p. 62.
18. See interview with António Delfim Neto in O'Shaughnessy, et al, "Financial," p. 20.
19. Economist Intelligence Unit, *QER: Brazil*, No. 1, 1973, p. 9.
20. Haq, "Employment," p. 2.
21. Brazil, *Plan*, pp. 53-54.
22. Ibid., p. 66.
23. Ibid., p. 62.
24. Ibid., pp. 63-66.
25. Economist Intelligence Unit, *QER: Brazil*, No. 1, 1973, pp. 5-6.
26. O'Shaughnessy, et al, "Financial," p. 21.
27. Ibid.
28. Economist Intelligence Unit, *QER: Brazil*, No. 1, 1973, p. 17.
29. Greenwald, "Enterprise," pp. 245-266.
30. ILO, *Full*, p. 114.
31. Ibid., pp. 167-168.
32. Nelson, Schultz, and Slighton, *Structural*, pp. 224-225.
33. Ibid., p. 312.
34. PREALC, *Creación*.
35. PREALC, *Costa Rica*, p. 150.
36. Business International, *Nationalism*, p. 24.
37. Morgan, "Transfer," pp. 143-144.
38. Grant, "Equal," p. 2.
39. See The United Mexican States, "Texto."
40. See OAS, "Document," p. 78.
41. ILO, *Full*, p. 163.
42. Baranson, "Multinational," p. 11.
43. Chung, "Property," pp. 29-34.
44. Utley, "Business," p. 80.
45. Gabriel, "Importing."
46. American Society of International Law, *Multinational*, p. 20.
47. See Ozawa, *Japan*, p. 8.
48. See findings of Scott, Little, and Scitovsky in Malmgren, *Trade*, p. 10.
49. Wallender, "Focus," p. 3.

CHAPTER VIII

1. Prebisch, *Change*, p. 2.
2. Olin, "Pressure," p. 142.
3. Ibid., p. 159.
4. See Bradford, *Forces*, preface.

BIBLIOGRAPHY

Abbott, Joan. "The Employment of Women and the Reduction of Fertility: Implications for Development." *World Development,* Vol. 2, No. 2. February 1974.

Agency for International Development, Office of Science and Technology. *Policies and Programs in Selected Areas of Science and Technology* (TA/OST 73-18). Washington, D.C.: AID, March 1973.

——. *Workshop on Science and Technology Priorities for International Development* (Conference at Airlie House, Warrenton, Virginia, December 17-19, 1971). Washington, D.C.: AID, 1972.

Alba, Victor. *Politics and the Labor Movement in Latin America.* Palo Alto, California: Stanford University Press, 1968.

Alexander, Robert J. *Organized Labor in Latin America.* New York: The Free Press, 1965.

Andean Common Market. *Andean Agreement of Subregional Integration* (Unofficial translation of the agreement establishing an Andean Common Market, signed in Bogota by Bolivia, Chile, Colombia, Ecuador, and Peru). May 23, 1969.

——. "Decision No. 24 of Andean Pact" (Unofficial translation supplied by the American Chamber of Commerce of Venezuela). March 1, 1973.

Baer, Werner, and Michel E. A. Hervé. "Employment and Industrialization in Developing Countries." *The Quarterly Journal of Economics,* Vol. 80, No. 1, February 1966.

Balasubramanyam, V. N. *International Transfer of Technology to India.* New York: Frederick A. Praeger, 1973.

Baranson, Jack. "The Changing Role of MNCs in Technological Advancement of LDCs." *Atlanta Economic Review,* Vol. 22, No. 9, September 1972.

——. "Employment Effects of Technology Programs in Developing Countries." *Technos,* Vol. 1, No. 4, October-December 1972.

——. "Multinational Corporations and Developing Country Goals for Technological Self-Sufficiency." Paper presented at Allied Social Science Association Meeting, Toronto, Canada, December 27, 1972. Mimeographed.

——. "National Efforts to Mobilize Technology in Support of Industrial Enterprise" (HBS 72-38). Graduate School of Business Administration, Harvard University, 1972.

——. *Industrial Technologies for Developing Economies.* New York: Frederick A. Praeger, 1969.

——. *International Transfer of Automotive Technology to Developing Countries.* UNITAR Research Report No. 8. New York: United Nations Institute for Training and Research, 1971.

——. *Manufacturing Problems in India: The Cummins Diesel Experience.* Syracuse, New York: Syracuse University Press, 1967.

Belli, R. David. "Plant and Equipment Expenditures by Foreign Affiliates of U.S. Corporations." *Survey of Current Business,* Vol. 52, No. 9, September 1972.

Blake, David H. "International Labor and the Regulation of Multinational Corporations: Proposals and Prospect." *The San Diego Law Review,* Vol. 11, No. 1, November 1973.

Bradford, Colin I. *Forces for Change in Latin America: U.S. Policy Implications.* Washington, D. C.: Overseas Development Council, 1971.

Business International Corporation. *The Andean Common Market* (1971 Supplement). New York: Business International Corporation, 1970.

——. *Brazil: New Business Power in Latin America.* New York: Business International Corporation, 1971.

——. *The Effects of U.S. Corporate Foreign Investment 1960-70.* New York: Business International Corporation, 1972.

——. *Financing Foreign Operations.* 2nd edition. New York: Business International Corporation, 1964.

——. *Nationalism in Latin America: The Challenge and Corporate Response.* New York: Business International Corporation, 1970.

——. *Using Latin America as an Export Base.* Management Monograph No. 56. New York: Business International Corporation, 1972.

——. *Venezuela: Business Problems and Opportunities.* New York: Business International Corporation, New York, 1968.

Chandavarkar, Anand G. "More Growth—More Employment?" *Finance and Development,* Vol. 9, No. 2, June 1972.

Chudson, Walter A. *The International Transfer of Commercial Technology to Developing Countries.* UNITAR Research Report No. 13. New York: United Nations Institute for Training and Research, 1971.

Chung, William K. "Property, Plant, and Equipment Expenditures by Majority-Owned Foreign Affiliates of U.S. Companies: Projections for 1974 and 1975." *Survey of Current Business,* Vol. 54, No. 9, September 1974.

Clague, Christopher. "The Determinants of Efficiency in Manufacturing Industries in an Underdeveloped Country." In *Workers and Managers in Latin America,* Stanley M. Davis and Louis Wolf Goodman (eds.). Lexington, Massachusetts: D. C. Heath & Company, 1972.

Clarke, Robin. *The Great Experiment: Science and Technology in the Second United Nations Development Decade.* New York: United Nations Center for Economic and Social Information, 1971.

——. "The Pressing Need for Alternative Technology." *Impact of Science on Society* (UNESCO), Vol. 23, No. 4, October-December 1973.

Cohen, Benjamin I., and Nathaniel H. Leff. "Employment and Industrialization: Comment." *The Quarterly Journal of Economics,* Vol. 81, No. 1, February 1967.

Council of the Americas. "The Effects of Foreign Investment on Latin America

BIBLIOGRAPHY

as a Whole, Argentina, Brazil, and Mexico." New York: The Council of the Americas, July 1972. Mimeographed.

——. *1972 Annual Report & 1973 Program.* New York: The Council of the Americas, 1973.

de la Torre, Jose R. "Foreign Investment and Export Dependency." Paper presented at the Conference on Latin America-United States Economic Interactions, March 18-21 1973, at University of Texas at Austin. Mimeographed.

Dennison, Charles S., "Latin American Technological Development and the Private Investor: The Issues and the Potential for Joint Activities." Paper presented at the Third Round Table on Foreign Private Investment in Latin America, Caracas, February 1973. Mimeographed.

——. "The Role of the International Productive Sector in Latin American Scientific and Technological Development: Observations and Proposals." Paper presented at CACTAL, Brasilia, May 1972. Mimeographed.

Economist Intelligence Unit. *Quarterly Economic Review: Argentina,* No. 1, 1973. London: The Economist Intelligence Unit, 1973.

——. *Quarterly Economic Review: Brazil,* Annual Supplement, 1972. London: The Economist Intelligence Unit, 1972.

——. *Quarterly Economic Review: Brazil,* No. 1, 1973. London: The Economist Intelligence Unit, 1973.

——. *Quarterly Economic Review: Colombia, Ecuador,* Annual Supplement, 1972. London: The Economist Intelligence Unit, 1972.

——. *Quarterly Economic Review: Mexico,* No. 1, 1973. London: The Economist Intelligence Unit, 1973.

——. *Quarterly Economic Review: Venezuela,* Annual Supplement, 1972. London: The Economist Intelligence Unit, 1972.

Edwards, Edgar O. "Employment in Developing Countries." In *Employment in Developing Nations,* Edgar O. Edwards (ed.). New York and London: Columbia University Press, 1974.

Federative Republic of Brazil. *First National Development Plan 1972/74.* Brasilia, November 1971.

Field, Arthur J. *Urbanization and Work in Modernizing Societies.* Detroit: Glengary Press, 1967.

Friedlin, J. N., and L. A. Lupo. "U.S. Direct Investment Abroad in 1973." *Survey of Current Business,* Vol. 54, No. 8, Part II, August 1974.

Fritsch, William R. *Progress and Profits: The Sears, Roebuck Story in Peru.* Washington, D. C.: Action Committee for International Development, 1962.

Furtado, Celso. "Political Obstacles to Economic Growth in Brazil." In *Obstacles to Change in Latin America,* Claudio Veliz (ed.). London: Oxford University Press, 1965.

Gabriel, Peter P. "Importing Corporate Capabilities without Exporting Ownership and Control: Alternatives to Foreign Direct Investment." Paper presented at the Conference on Latin America-United States Economic Interactions, University of Texas at Austin, March 18-21, 1973. Mimeographed.

Galenson, Walter. "Economic Development and the Sectoral Expansion of Employment." *International Labour Review,* Vol. 88, No. 6, June 1963.

Giral, José B., and Robert P. Morgan (co-directors). *Appropriate Technology for Chemical Industries in Developing Countries.* A report prepared in connection with the Foreign Area Fellowship Program, Summer Research Training Project, National Autonomous University of Mexico, Mexico City, July-August 1972.

Goodman, Louis Wolf. "The Unequal Distribution of Income in Latin America."

BIBLIOGRAPHY

In *Workers and Managers in Latin America,* Stanley M. Davis and Louis Wolf Goodman (eds.). Lexington, Massachusetts: D. C. Heath & Company, 1972.

Grant, James P. "Accelerating Progress through Social Justice." *International Development Review,* Vol. 14, No. 3, September 1972.

——. "Equal Access and Participation vs. Trickle Down and Redistribution: The Welfare Issue for Low-Income Societies." Prepared for One Asia Assembly 1973, New Delhi, India, February 5-7, 1973. Washington, D. C.: Overseas Development Council, 1973. Mimeographed.

——. "Multinational Corporations and the Developing Countries: The Emerging Jobs Crisis and its Implications." Washington, D.C.: Overseas Development Council, January 1972. Mimeographed.

Greenwald, Dennis L. "The Multinational Enterprise in the Context of Latin American Economic Integration: The Andean Agreement Model." *The San Diego Law Review,* Vol. 11, No. 1, November 1973.

Gurley, John G. "Rural Development in China, 1949-1972, and the Lessons to be Learned from It." In *Employment in Developing Nations,* Edgar O. Edwards (ed.). New York and London: Columbia University Press, 1974.

Hagen, Everett E. *The Economics of Development.* Homewood, Illinois: Richard D. Irwin, 1968.

Haissman, I. "Rural Industrialization in Mexico: A Case Study." Paper presented at Expert Group Meeting on Rural Industrialization (United Nations, ESA/SD/AC.5/9), Bucharest, September 24-28, 1973. Mimeographed.

Hall, O. Milton. "Attitudes and Unemployment: A Comparison of the Opinions and Attitudes of Employed and Unemployed Men." *Archives of Psychology,* No. 165. New York: Columbia University, March 1934.

Haq, Mahbub ul. "Employment in the 1970s: A New Perspective." *Perspectives on Development.* Reprint, New York: The Agricultural Development Council, October 1972.

Hellinger, Doug, and Steve Hellinger. "Sectoral Analysis of Employment-Generation Potential in Latin America." Washington, D.C.: 1973. Mimeographed.

Higgins, Benjamin. *Economic Development: Principles, Problems, and Policies,* New York: W. W. Norton, 1959.

Hirshman, Albert O. *The Strategy of Economic Development.* New Haven, Connecticut: Yale University Press, 1958.

Hoda, Mansur. "Development Is a Two-Way Street Toward Survival." *Impact of Science on Society* (UNESCO), Vol. 23, No. 4, October-December 1973.

International Labour Office. *Employment, Incomes and Equality: A Strategy for Increasing Productive Employment in Kenya.* Geneva: International Labour Office, 1972.

——. *Towards Full Employment: A Programme for Colombia.* Geneva: International Labour Office, 1970.

Jackson, Sarah. "Economically Appropriate Technologies for Developing Countries: A Survey." Paper prepared for the National Academy of Sciences. Washington, D.C.: Overseas Development Council, December 1971.

Johnson, Harry. "The Multinational Corporation as a Development Agent." *Columbia Journal of World Business,* Vol. 5, No. 3, May-June 1970.

Jones, Gavin W. "Underutilization of Manpower and Demographic Trends in Latin America." In *Workers and Managers in Latin America,* Stanley M. Davis and Louis Wolf Goodman (eds.). Lexington, Massachusetts: D.C. Heath & Company, 1972.

Juma, Omari S., and Guy Routh. "Automated Production of Cans in Tanzania."

In *Automation in Developing Countries.* Geneva: International Labour Office, 1972.

Junta de Planificación (Puerto Rico). *Informe Económico al Gobernador 1969.* San Juan: Estado Libre Asociado de Puerto Rico, January 1970.

Keremitsis, Dawn. "Women Textile Workers in Mexico and Colombia." Paper presented at the Congreso Internacional de Americanistas, Mexico City, September, 1974. Mimeographed.

Khan, Amir V. "Appropriate Technologies: Do We Transfer, Adapt, or Develop?" In *Employment in Developing Nations,* Edgar O. Edwards (ed.). New York and London: Columbia University Press, 1974.

Kreinin, Mordechai E. "Comparative Labor Effectiveness." *American Economic Review,* Vol. 55, No. 1, March 1965.

Lauterbach, Albert. *Enterprise in Latin America: Business Attitudes in a Developing Economy.* Ithaca, New York: Cornell University Press, 1966.

Leff, Nathaniel H. "Investment in the LDCs: The Next Wave." *Columbia Journal of World Business,* Vol. 4, No. 6, November-December 1969.

MacEoin, Gary. *Revolution Next Door: Latin America in the 1970s.* New York: Holt, Rinehart and Winston, 1971.

McMillan, Jr., Claude and Richard F. González, with Leo G. Erikson, *International Enterprise in a Developing Economy: A Study of U.S. Business in Brazil.* East Lansing, Michigan: Michigan State University, 1964.

McNamara, Robert S. "Address to the Board of Governors (of IBRD)." Washington, D.C., September 29, 1969.

Macrae, Norman. "The Future of International Business." *The Economist,* Vol. 242, No. 6700, January 22, 1972.

Malmgren, Harald B. *Trade and Investment Relations between Developed and Developing Nations: A Review of the State of Knowledge.* Washington, D.C.: Overseas Development Council, 1971.

Margolies, Daniel. "Multinational Corporations and Adaptive Research for Developing Countries." *Appropriate Technologies for International Development: Preliminary Survey of Research Activities* (TA/OST 72-11). Washington, D.C.: Agency for International Development, September 1972.

Marsden, Keith. "Progressive Technologies for Developing Countries." *International Labour Review,* Vol. 101, No. 5, May 1970.

Mason, R. Hal. *The Transfer of Technology and the Factor Proportions Problems: The Philippines and Mexico.* UNITAR Research Report No. 10, New York: United Nations Institute for Training and Research, 1970.

Morawetz, David. "Employment Implications of Industrialisation in Developing Countries: A Survey." *The Economic Journal,* Vol. 84, No. 335, September 1974.

Morgan, Robert P. "Transfer of Technology." Reprinted from *Changing Latin America: New Interpretations of Its Politics and Society,* Douglas A. Chalmers (ed.). Proceedings of the Academy of Political Science, August 1972.

——. "The Multinational Corporation and World Economic Development." *Journal of International Law,* Vol. 66, No. 4, Washington, D.C.: September 1972. (Proceedings).

National Academy of Sciences, Office of the Foreign Secretary. *U.S. International Firms and R, D & E in Developing Countries.* Washington, D.C.: National Academy of Sciences, 1973.

Nelson, Richard R., T. Paul Schultz, and Robert L. Slighton. *Structural Change in a Developing Economy: Colombia's Problems and Prospects.* Princeton, New

BIBLIOGRAPHY

Jersey: Princeton University Press, 1971.

Olin, Ulla. "Population Pressure and Revolutionary Movements." In *The Emotional Stress of War, Violence, and Peace,* Rolland S. Parker (ed.). New York: Stanwix House, 1972.

Organization of American States, Department of Scientific Affairs, General Secretariat. *General Description of the Organization of American States' Pilot Project for Transfer of Technology.* Washington, D.C.: Organization of American States, 1972.

——. "OAS Programs Related to Science and Technology" (OEA/Ser.K/XVIII.1, CACTAL/doc. 131). Prepared for the Meeting of the Group of Governmental Experts. Washington, D.C.: Organization of American States, August 18, 1972.

——. "Working Document" for CACTAL (OEA/Ser. K/XVIII.1, CACTAL/doc. 5, rev. 1). Washington, D.C.: Organization of American States, April 20, 1972.

——. *Science, Technology, and Development: The Concensus of Brasilia* (Summary of CACTAL). Washington, D.C.: Organization of American States, October 1972.

——. *Specialized Conference on the Application of Science and Technology to Latin American Development: Final Report* (CACTAL, May 12–19, 1972, Brasilia, Brazil). Washington, D.C.: Organization of American States, 1972.

O'Shaughnessy, Hugh, Emanuel de Kadt, and Sarita Kendall. "Financial Times Survey: Brazil." *The Financial Times,* London. October 10, 1972.

Owens, Edgar and Robert d'A. Shaw. *Development Reconsidered.* Lexington, Massachusetts: D.C. Heath & Company, 1972.

Ozawa, Terutomo. *Transfer of Technology from Japan to Developing Countries.* UNITAR Research Report No. 7, New York: United Nations Institute for Training and Research, 1971.

Pack, Howard. "The Use of Labor-Intensive Techniques in Kenyan Industry." In *Technology and Economics in International Development: Report of a Seminar* (TA/OST 72-9). Washington, D.C.: Agency for International Development, May 1972.

Pickett, James, D. J. C. Forsyth, and N. S. McBain. "The Choice of Technology, Economic Efficiency and Employment in Developing Countries." In *Employment in Developing Nations,* Edgar O. Edwards (ed.). New York and London: Columbia University Press, 1974.

Poats, Rutherford M. *Technology for Developing Nations,* Washington, D.C.: The Brookings Institution, 1972.

Prebisch, Raúl. *Change and Development: Latin America's Great Task.* Washington, D.C.: Inter-American Development Bank, 1970.

Programa Regional del Empleo para América Latina y el Caribe. *Creación de Empleos y Absorción del Desempleo en Chile.* Geneva: International Labour Office, 1972.

——. *Situación y Perspectivas del Empleo en Costa Rica.* Geneva: International Labour Office, 1972.

Ramos, Joseph R. *Labor and Development in Latin America.* New York: Columbia University Press, 1968.

Ranis, Gustav, "Factor Proportions in Japanese Economic Development." *The American Economic Review,* Vol. 47, No. 5, September 1957.

——. "Industrial Sector Labor Absorption." *Economic Development and Cultural Change,* Vol. 21, No. 3, April 1973.

——. "Some Observations on the Economic Framework for Optimum LDC Utilization of Technology." In *Technology and Economics in International Develop-*

ment: *Report of a Seminar* (TA/OST 72-9). Washington, D.C.: Agency for International Development, May 1972.

Reynolds, Lloyd G., and Peter Gregory. *Wages, Productivity, and Industrialization in Puerto Rico.* Homewood, Illinois: Richard D. Irwin, Inc., 1965.

Rich, William. *Smaller Families through Social and Economic Progress.* Washington, D.C.: Overseas Development Council, January 1973.

Rosenstein-Rodan, Paul N. "Problems of Private Foreign Investment and Multinational Corporations." Paper presented at the Conference on Latin America-United States Economic Interactions, University of Texas at Austin, March 18-21, 1973. Mimeographed.

Sabolo, Yves. "Sectoral Employment Growth: The Outlook for 1980." *International Labour Review.* Vol. 100, No. 5, November 1969.

Shapiro, Harvey D. "Giants Beyond Flag and Country." *The New York Times Magazine,* March 18, 1973.

Shaw, Robert d'A. *Rethinking Economic Development.* Washington, D.C.: Overseas Development Council, March 1972.

Shaw, Robert d'A. and Donald R. Sherk. "The International Utilization of Labor and the Multinational Corporation in the Pacific Basin." In *Pacific Basin Development: The American Interests.* Harald B. Malmgren (ed.). Lexington, Massachusetts: D.C. Heath & Company, 1972.

Sigurdson, Jon. "Technology and Employment in China." Paper prepared for Ford Foundation Seminar on Technology and Employment, New Delhi, March 21-24, 1973.

Slawinski, Zygmundt. "Prospects of Structural Changes in Employment in Latin America." In *Workers and Managers in Latin America,* Stanley M. Davis and Louis Wolf Goodman (eds.). Lexington, Massachusetts: D.C. Heath & Company, 1972.

Stanford Research Institute. *Manual of Industrial Development with Special Application to Latin America.* Washington, D.C.: Foreign Operations Administration, May 1955.

Strassmann, W. Paul. "The Industrialist and Labor." In *Workers and Managers in Latin America.* Stanley M. Davis and Louis Wolf Goodman (eds.). Lexington, Massachusetts: D.C. Heath & Company, 1972.

——. *Technological Change and Economic Development: The Manufacturing Experience of Mexico and Puerto Rico.* Ithaca, New York: Cornell University Press, 1968.

Sunkel, Osvaldo. "Big Business and 'Dependencia'—A Latin American View." *Foreign Affairs,* Vol. 50, No. 3, April 1972.

Tarapore, Savak S. "Transmission of Technology to Developing Countries." *Finance and Development,* Vol. 9, No. 2, June 1972.

Thorbecke, Erik. "The Employment Problem: A Critical Evaluation of Four ILO Comprehensive Country Reports." *International Labour Review,* Vol. 107, No. 5, May 1973.

——. "Unemployment and Underemployment in the Developing World." Paper prepared for the Columbia University Conference on International Economic Development, Williamsburg, Virginia, and New York, February 1970. Mimeographed.

Turner, Louis. *Multinational Companies and the Third World.* New York: Hill and Wang, 1973.

United Mexican States. "Texto de la Iniciativa de Ley sobre el Registro de la Transferencia de Technología." Mexico City: Secretariat of Industry and Commerce,

BIBLIOGRAPHY

November 3, 1972.

United Nations. *The Impact of Multinational Corporations on the Development Process and on International Relations* (E/74/II.A.5;ST/5500/REV.1). New York: United Nations, 1974.

United Nations, Department of Economic and Social Affairs. *Panel on Foreign Investment in Latin America* (Medellin, Colombia, June 8-11, 1970). New York: United Nations, 1971.

United Nations Industrial Development Organization. *Textile Industry.* UNIDO Monograph No. 7, New York: United Nations, 1969.

——. *Chemical Industry.* UNIDO Monograph No. 8, N.Y.: United Nations, 1969.

——. *Industrial Research.* UNIDO Monograph No. 10, N.Y.: United Nations, 1969.

——. *Small-Scale Industry in Latin America.* UNIDO Monograph No. 11, New York: United Nations, 1969.

——. *Estimation of Managerial and Technical Personnel Requirements in Selected Industries.* Training for Industry Series No. 2, New York: United Nations, 1968.

United States Bureau of Labor Statistics. "Labor Force Participation Rates in Latin America." In *Workers and Managers in Latin America*, Stanley M. Davis and Louis Wolf Goodman (eds.). Lexington, Massachusetts: D.C. Heath & Company, 1972.

Urquidi, Victor L. "Some Implications of Foreign Investment for Latin America." In *Obstacles to Change in Latin America.* Claudio Veliz (ed.). London: Oxford University Press, 1965.

Utley, John Basil. "Doing Business with Latin Nationalists." *Harvard Business Review*, Vol. 51, No. 1, January-February 1973.

Vaitsos, Constantine V. "Employment Effects of Foreign Direct Investments in Developing Countries." In *Employment in Developing Nations*, Edgar O. Edwards (ed.). New York and London: Columbia University Press, 1974.

van Houten, Jan. "Assembly Industries in the Caribbean." *Finance and Development*, Vol. 10, No. 2, June 1973

Vernon, Raymond. *Sovereignty at Bay: The Multinational Spread of U.S. Enterprises.* New York and London: Basic Books, 1971.

Wallender, III, Harvey W. "A Changing Focus in Latin America for U.S. Business." New York: The Council of the Americas, 1973. Mimeographed.

Weed, Stephen J. "Some Economic Considerations for Developing-Country Technologies." Bureau for Program and Policy Coordination, Office of Policy Development and Analysis, Agency for International Development, Washington, D.C., December 1971.

Wells, Jr., Louis T. "Economic Man and Engineering Man: Choice of Technology in a Low Wage Country." Economic Development Report No. 226, Cambridge, Mass: Development Research Group, Center for International Affairs, Harvard University, November 1972. Mimeographed.

Williams, Simon. "Organization of a Textile Industry—Costs and Benefits to the Economy." *Industrial Development: Science, Technology, and Development*, United States Papers prepared for the United Nations Conference on the Application of Science and Technology for the Benefits of the Less Developed Areas, Vol. IV. Washington, D.C., 1963.

Wood, Richardson, and Virginia Keyser. *Sears, Roebuck de México, S. A.*, Washington D.C.: National Planning Association, 1953.

Zschock, Dieter K. *Manpower Perspective of Colombia.* Princeton, New Jersey: Industrial Relations Section, Princeton University, 1967.

INDEX